My FIRST OXFORD Dictionary

Compiled by Evelyn Goldsmith

Illustrated by Julie Park

Oxford University Press

My name is _____

Oxford University Press, Walton Street, Oxford OX2 6DP

Oxford   New York
Athens   Auckland   Bangkok   Bombay
Calcutta   Cape Town   Dar es Salaam   Delhi
Florence   Hong Kong   Istanbul   Karachi
Kuala Lumpur   Madras   Madrid   Melbourne
Mexico City   Nairobi   Paris   Singapore
Taipei   Tokyo   Toronto

and associated companies in
Berlin   Ibadan

Oxford is a trade mark of Oxford University Press

© Oxford University Press 1993
First published in 1993
7 9 10 8 6

ISBN 0 19 910236 8 (net hardback)
ISBN 0 19 910275 9 (net paperback)

A CIP catalogue record for this book is available from the British Library

Designed by
Shireen Nathoo Design
Typeset by
Pentacor PLC, High Wycombe, Bucks
Printed in Great Britain by
Butler & Tanner Ltd, Frome and London

INTRODUCTION

My First Oxford Dictionary is a lively, colourful dictionary for children aged five years upwards. The selection of entries is based on extensive classroom research into words young children frequently come across in their reading, and use in their writing and speaking. Younger readers will use this dictionary to see how familiar words are spelt, while more confident readers will look up a word for meaning.

Over 550 colour illustrations have been carefully chosen to suit the needs of children. They are beautifully drawn and entertaining, so that the very young will enjoy looking at the pictures and then progress to matching them to familiar words. Older children will find the illustrations indispensable when tackling new words and understanding written definitions. All illustrations are accurate and precise, and serve an important purpose in leading children to interpreting dictionary entries correctly.

This dictionary also introduces children to simple grammar. It helps them to recognize that some words have plurals

frog   (frogs)

some change their endings according to their tense

ask   (asking, asked)

and others have comparative and superlative forms

bad   (worse, worst)

They may also discover that a word can have several meanings

chest   (chests)
1   A big, strong box
2   The top part of your body

or that the same word can be used in quite different ways

drop ¹   (drops)
A tiny amount of liquid
drop ²   (dropping, dropped)
If you drop something you let it fall

My First Oxford Dictionary will develop early dictionary skills, as well as an interest in the English language. **A first book of words for children to treasure!**

★
1,500 headwords in colour clearly and simply defined
★
Example sentences to illustrate use and explain meaning
★
The alphabet down the outer side of every page to help young readers with alphabetical word order
★
A list of words we often use, such as *and, but, to, she*, which cannot be illustrated and which would not necessarily be looked up for meaning
★

Special Picture Section
Here you will find more colour illustrations with identifying labels. Look for:

Colours and Shapes
Opposites
Fruit
Vegetables
Flowers
Trees
Animals in the Wild
Dinosaurs
Farm Animals
Pets
Your Body
Transport
Time
Seasons
Days
Months
Numbers

Aa

b c d e f g h i j k l m n o p q r s t u v w x y z

accident (accidents)
An accident is something nasty that was not meant to happen.
Tom broke his arm in a car accident.

ache (aching, ached)
If part of your body aches, it goes on hurting.
That long bicycle ride has made my legs ache.

active
When you are active, you move quickly and do a lot of things.
Those children at the playground are so active they never sit still.

add (adding, added)
1 When you add something, you put it with something else.
Mix the eggs and sugar. Then add flour.
2 When you add, you find the answer to a sum like this:

$$6 + 6 = ?$$

address (addresses)
Someone's address is the number of their house, and the name of the street and town where they live.

Mr and Mrs Adrian Smith
132 High Street
Oxford
OX1 5BC

adult (adults)
An adult is a person or animal that has grown up.

adventure (adventures)
An adventure is something exciting that happens to you.

aeroplane (aeroplanes)
An aeroplane is a flying machine with wings, and one or more engines.

afraid
Someone who is afraid thinks something bad might happen to them.
Sarah was afraid to jump into the pool.

afternoon (afternoons)
The afternoon is the time from the middle of the day until about six o'clock.

against
If you are against somebody, you are on the opposite side to them.
When we play against you, we shall win.

age
The age of someone or something is how old they are.

4

air
Air is what everyone breathes.

airport (airports)
An airport is a place where aeroplanes land and take off, and people go to travel.

alive
A person, animal, or plant that is alive is living at the moment.

allow (allowing, allowed)
If you are allowed to do something, you may do it.
I am allowed out today because it is not raining.

almost
Almost means very nearly.
We almost missed the bus.

alone
If someone is alone, there is nobody with them.
Our puppy cries if he is left alone.

alphabet (alphabets)
An alphabet is all the letters that are used in writing, arranged in a special order. a b c d e f g h i j k l m n o p q r s t u v w x y z

always
If something always happens, it happens every time.
I am always awake by six o'clock.

ambulance (ambulances)
An ambulance is a special van for taking people to hospital when they are injured or ill.

amphibian (amphibians)
Amphibians are animals that start their lives in water and later change so they are able to live on land. Frogs are amphibians.

ancient
Things that are ancient are very old.

angry (angrier, angriest)
If you are angry, you feel upset and want to fight or shout crossly.
Dad was angry when I broke the window.

animal (animals)
An animal is something that lives, can move about, and is not a plant. Parrots, elephants, bees, goldfish, and people are all animals.

ankle (ankles)
Your ankle is the part where your leg joins your foot.

Aa
b c d e f g h i j k l m n o p q r s t u v w x y z

5

Aa

b c d e f g h i j k l m n o p q r s t u v w x y z

announce (announcing, announced)
If people announce something, they tell everyone about it.
The teacher announced that she was leaving at the end of term.

annoy (annoying, annoyed)
If someone annoys you, they make you angry.
William annoyed his parents by banging the door every time he went out.

answer (answering, answered)
Answering is speaking when someone calls you or asks you a question.
Daniel's mother called him, but it was some time before he answered.

ant (ants)
An ant is a tiny insect. Ants live in large groups called colonies.

anxious
If you are anxious, you feel worried about something.
Mum gets anxious when I am late home.

ape (apes)
An ape is an animal like a large monkey without a tail. Chimpanzees are apes.

appear (appearing, appeared)
If something appears, you can suddenly see it.
The door opened and Dad appeared.

apple (apples)
An apple is a round, crisp fruit. Apples have green, red, or yellow skins.

area (areas)
An area is part of a country or a place.
There are good schools in this area.

argue (arguing, argued)
When you argue with somebody, you talk about things you do not agree on.
My brother never agrees with me so we always argue.

arm (arms)
Your arm is between your shoulder and your hand.

armchair (armchairs)
An armchair is a comfortable chair with parts at the side for you to rest your arms on.

arrange (arranging, arranged)
If you arrange things, you put them in order.
Arrange the books in neat piles.

art

Art is something special that someone has made, like a drawing, painting, or carving.

ask (asking, asked)

1 When you ask a question, you are trying to find something out.
I asked how old their baby was.
2 If you ask for something, you say you want it to be given to you.
I asked for a bar of chocolate.

asleep

When you are asleep, you are resting completely, with your eyes closed, and you don't know what is going on around you.

assembly (assemblies)

Assembly is the time when a large group of people meet together.
I was late for assembly at school this morning.

ate

See **eat**.
My sister ate too much at the party.

attention

1 If somebody or something attracts your attention, you notice them.
Flashing lights attracted my attention.
2 When you pay attention to somebody, you think about what they are saying.
James, stop talking and pay attention.

attract (attracting, attracted)

1 If something attracts a person or animal, they become interested in it.
Shiny things attract jackdaws.
2 When a magnet attracts something, it makes it come nearer.

audience (audiences)

An audience is a group of people who have come to a place to see or hear something.
At the end of the play the audience clapped loudly.

autumn (autumns)

Autumn is the part of the year when it gets colder, and leaves fall from the trees.

awkward

Something awkward is difficult to use.
The toy cupboard is in an awkward place. I can't reach it.

Aa
b c d e f g h i j k l m n o p q r s t u v w x y z

bag (bags)
A bag is used to hold or carry things.

baby (babies)
A baby is a very young child.

back (backs)
1 The back of something is the part opposite to the front.
John ran out of the back door.
2 The back of a person or animal is the part between the neck and the bottom or tail.

bad (worse, worst)
1 Things that are bad are not good.
Sweets are bad for your teeth.
2 Bad food is not fit to eat.
I can't eat that egg. It's bad.

bake (baking, baked)
When you bake something, you cook it in an oven.
My dad is baking some cakes.

balance (balancing, balanced)
When you balance something, you keep it steady.
Polly can balance four books on her head.

ball (balls)
A ball is a round object that is used in games.

balloon (balloons)
A balloon is a small, coloured rubber bag that you can blow into and make bigger.

8

banana   (bananas)
A banana is a long fruit
with a thick, yellow skin.

band   (bands)
1   A band is a group of people who
play musical instruments together.
We are going to hear a band play.
2   A band can also be a strip of
material round something.
*You can keep your pencils together with a
rubber band.*

bank   (banks)
1   A bank is a place that looks
after money and valuable things
for people.
2   A bank is also the ground near the
edge of a river, canal, or lake.

bar   (bars)
A bar is a long, thin piece of wood
or metal.
*The monkey put its hand through the bars
of its cage.*

bare   (barer, barest)
1   If part of someone's body is bare,
it is not covered.
Jenny came downstairs in her bare feet.
2   A room or cupboard that is bare
has nothing in it.

bargain   (bargains)
A bargain is something that is worth
more than you pay for it.
I got a real bargain in the sale.

bark [1]
Bark is the hard covering round the
trunk and branches of a tree.

bark [2]   (barking, barked)
When dogs and foxes bark, they make
a hard, loud sound.

barn   (barns)
A barn is a large building on a farm,
used to store things like hay.

basket   (baskets)
A basket is for holding or carrying
things. Baskets are made of strips of
material like straw or thin wood.

bat   (bats)
1   A bat is a piece of wood for
hitting the ball in a game.
2   A bat is also an
animal like a mouse
with wings.

bath   (baths)
A bath can be filled with water so that
you can sit in it and wash yourself.

bathroom   (bathrooms)
A room with a bath or shower.

battery   (batteries)
A battery has electricity inside it. You
put batteries in things like torches
and radios to make them work.
My watch needs a new battery.

a b c d e f g h i j k l m n o p q r s t u v w x y z

Bb

beach (beaches)
A beach is land by the edge of the sea. It is usually covered with sand or small stones.

beak (beaks)
A beak is the hard part round a bird's mouth.
The bird had some twigs in its beak.

bear (bears)
A bear is a big, heavy animal with very thick fur.

beard (beards)
A beard is the hair that grows on a man's chin.
The wizard had a long, white beard.

beat (beating, beaten)
1 If you beat someone in a race, you go faster than they do.
I ran very fast, but Alex beat me.
2 To beat can also mean to keep hitting with a stick.
Don't let him beat the donkey.

beautiful
You say someone or something is beautiful if you enjoy looking at them or listening to them.
A blackbird's song is beautiful.

bed (beds)
A bed is something to lie down on.
It's time you were in bed.

bedroom (bedrooms)
A bedroom is a room you sleep in.

bee (bees)
A bee is an insect with wings. Bees make honey.

beetle (beetles)
A beetle is an insect with hard wing-covers.

began
See **begin**.
Tom began to talk when he was two.

begin (beginning, begun)
When you begin, you start something.
Begin running when I blow the whistle.

begun
See **begin**.
I have just begun a new drawing.

behave (behaving, behaved)
If someone tells you to behave, they want you to be good.

10

behind

Behind means at the back of something.

David hid behind a bush.

believe (believing, believed)

If you believe something, you feel sure it is true.

Her little brother believes in fairies.

bell (bells)

A bell is a piece of metal that makes a ringing sound when it is hit.

belong (belonging, belonged)

1 If something belongs to somebody, it is theirs.

That pencil belongs to me.

2 If you belong to something, you are part of it.

My brother belongs to the Scouts.

3 If something belongs somewhere, that is its proper place.

Where does this book belong?

belt (belts)

A belt is a band that you wear round your waist.

Your belt needs to be tighter – your jeans keep slipping down.

bend (bending, bent)

If you bend something, you stop it being straight.

Bend your knees, then straighten them.

bent

See **bend**.

The teacher bent a piece of wire into a circle.

best

Something or somebody that is the best is better than any of the others.

Yours is the best drawing today, Mark.

better

1 If someone can do something better than you, they are cleverer than you are at it.

Alice can draw better than I can.

2 If one thing is better than another, it is more useful, or nearer to what you want.

Your red jumper would be better – it's warmer.

3 If you are feeling better, you are well again.

bicycle (bicycles)

A bicycle is a machine that you can ride. Bicycles have two wheels. A bicycle is often called a bike for short.

saddle handlebars
chain wheel
pedal spokes

big (bigger, biggest)

Somebody or something big is large.

I am much bigger than my baby sister.

a **Bb** c d e f g h i j k l m n o p q r s t u v w x y z

11

Bb

bike (bikes)
See **bicycle**.

bin (bins)
A bin is something to put things in.
You can use bins to store things like
bread or flour. Some bins are
for rubbish.

bird (birds)
A bird is an animal that has wings,
feathers, and a beak.

birthday (birthdays)
Your birthday is a special day of the
year. It is remembered because it was
the day you were born on.

biscuit (biscuits)
A biscuit is a kind of small, thin,
dry cake.

bit
See **bite**.
Sam bit the apple with his new front teeth.

bite (biting, bitten)
If you bite something,
you use your teeth
to cut into it.

bitten
See **bite**.
The parrot has bitten my finger.

blade (blades)
A blade is the flat, sharp part of a
knife or sword.

blame (blaming, blamed)
If you blame someone, you think it is
because of them that something bad
has happened.
Mum blamed me for making the room a mess.

blanket (blankets)
A blanket is a thick cover for a bed.

blew
See **blow**.
Amy blew out all the candles at once.

blind 1
Someone who is blind
cannot see at all.

blind 2 (blinds)
A blind pulls down to cover a window.

block 1 (blocks)
A block is a thick piece of something
solid like wood or stone.

12

block [2]   (blocking, blocked)
If something is blocked, things cannot get through.
Leaves blocked the drain.

blood
Blood is the red liquid that moves round inside your body.

blow   (blowing, blown)
1   When you blow, you make air come out of your mouth.
Watch me blow bubbles!
2   When a wind blows, it moves the air.
The wind blew the leaves into a corner.

blown
See **blow**.
I've already blown the balloons up.

blunt   (blunter, bluntest)
Something like a knife or a pencil that is blunt is not sharp.

boat   (boats)
A boat floats and carries people or things on water.

body   (bodies)
The body of a person or animal is the whole of them.
His body was covered in spots.

boil   (boiling, boiled)
1   When water boils, it is very hot and you can see bubbles and steam.
2   When you boil something, you cook it in boiling water.
Now boil the potatoes.

bone   (bones)
Your bones are the hard parts inside your body.

bonfire   (bonfires)
A bonfire is a fire that someone lights outdoors.

book   (books)
A book has pages fixed inside a cover. Books may have writing and pictures in them.
I am reading a book about horses.

boot   (boots)
1   A boot is a kind of shoe that also covers your ankle.
Michael can't find his winter boots.
2   A boot is also the place in a car where you put luggage.
Put your skateboard in the boot.

a
Bb
c d e f g h i j k l m n o p q r s t u v w x y z

bored
If you are bored, you feel tired or irritated because you have nothing interesting to do.

born
When a baby is born, it begins to live outside its mother.
Our new baby was born last week.

borrow (borrowing, borrowed)
When you borrow something from somebody, they let you take it for a short time.
Can I borrow your pencil?

bottle (bottles)
A bottle is made to hold liquids.
There is a bottle of milk on the step.

bottom
The bottom is the lowest part of anything, and also the part of your body that you sit on.
Claire stood at the bottom of the stairs.

bought
See **buy**.
My dad has bought me a new bicycle.

bounce (bouncing, bounced)
When something bounces, it springs back.
The ball bounced off the wall.

bowl (bowls)
A bowl is a kind of deep plate that is made to hold things like soup, fruit, or breakfast cereals.
Christopher poured milk into his bowl.

box (boxes)
A box is made to hold things. Boxes are usually made from cardboard, wood, or plastic.

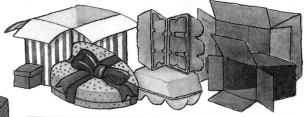

boy (boys)
A boy is a male child or young adult.

brain (brains)
Your brain is inside your head. You use your brain for thinking, remembering, and feeling.

branch (branches)
A branch grows out from the trunk of a tree.
Caroline swung from a low branch.

brave (braver, bravest)
If you are brave, you show that you are not afraid.
This might hurt a bit — you will have to be brave.

bread
Bread is a food made with flour.

break (breaking, broken)
If something breaks, it goes into pieces or stops working.
Don't break the window with that ball.

breakfast   (breakfasts)
Breakfast is the first meal after you wake up in the morning.

breathe   (breathing, breathed)
When you breathe, you take air in through your nose or mouth and send it out again.
When Lauren reached the top of the hill, she was breathing hard.

brick   (bricks)
A brick is a small block of baked clay. Bricks are used for building.

bridge   (bridges)
Bridges go over rivers, railways, or roads, so that people or traffic can get across.

bright   (brighter, brightest)
1   Bright colours are strong and easy to see.
2   Bright lights shine strongly.
3   A person who is bright learns quickly.

bring   (bringing, brought)
If you bring something, you carry it here.
Will you please bring money for the school trip tomorrow.

broke
See **break**.
I dropped my glass and it broke.

broken
See **break**.
The baby has broken my new mug.

broom   (brooms)

A broom is a brush for sweeping a path or floor. Brooms have long handles.

brought
See **bring**.
I have brought you some flowers.

brush   (brushes)
A brush has lots of short, stiff hairs, fixed into something like wood or plastic. There are brushes for things like making your hair tidy, or for painting.

bubble   (bubbles)
A bubble is a small ball of soap or liquid with air inside.
The fizzy drink was full of bubbles.

bucket   (buckets)
Buckets are used to carry liquids.

a
Bb
c d e f g h i j k l m n o p q r s t u v w x y z

15

Bb

a c d e f g h i j k l m n o p q r s t u v w x y z

build (building, built)
If you build something, you make it by putting parts together.
I'm building a castle with my blocks.

building (buildings)
A building has walls and a roof. Houses, factories, and schools are all buildings.

built
See **build**.
A robin built a nest in the old tree.

bulb (bulbs)
1 A bulb is the part of a lamp that gives light.
The bulb in my reading lamp has gone.
2 A bulb can be the root of a flower. Daffodils and tulips grow from bulbs.

burn (burning, burnt or burned)
1 If someone burns something, they damage it with fire or heat.
My mother burnt the toast.
2 If something is burning, it is on fire.
The bonfire burned brightly.

burst (bursting, burst)
When something bursts, it breaks open suddenly.
The bag burst and all the shopping fell on the floor.

bus (buses)
Buses are big vehicles that can carry lots of people to and from places.

bush (bushes)
A bush is like a small tree, with lots of branches.

busy (busier, busiest)
1 Someone who is busy has a lot to do.
Don't talk to Dad now – he's busy.
2 When a place is busy, there is a lot going on.
The supermarket was busy today.

butter
Butter is a yellow fat which is made from cream. You can spread it on bread or cook with it.

butterfly (butterflies)
A butterfly is an insect with four large white or coloured wings.

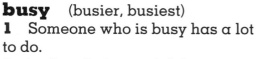

button (buttons)
Buttons are sewn on to clothes. They fit into holes or loops to keep the clothes done up.

buy (buying, bought)
When you buy something, you pay money to have it.
I would like to buy an ice cream.

16

cage (cages)

A cage is a box or room with bars. Pets like mice and gerbils live in cages.

cake (cakes)

A cake is food made with flour, butter, eggs, and sugar.

calculator (calculators)

A calculator is a machine that can do sums.

calendar (calendars)

A calendar is a list showing all the days, weeks, and months in a year.

call (calling, called)

1 If you call someone, you speak loudly so that they will come to you. *Didn't you hear me call you?*

2 If a person or thing is called something, that is their name. *Our dog is called Bumble.*

camel (camels)

A camel is a big animal with one or two humps on its back. Camels can carry people and things across deserts.

camera (cameras)

You use a camera to take photos.

a b Cc d e f g h i j k l m n o p q r s t u v w x y z

17

camp (camps)
A camp is a group of tents or huts where people live for a short time.
Can we go to a camp for our holiday?

candle (candles)
A candle is a stick of wax with string through it. You can set the string on fire and it gives light.

car (cars)
You can ride in a car. It has wheels and an engine to make it go.
My dad goes to work in the car.

caravan (caravans)
A caravan is a house on wheels. It can be pulled from place to place by a car or truck.
We are taking our caravan to the sea.

card (cards)
1 Card is thick, stiff paper.
2 A greetings card can have a picture and words on it.
You can send cards to people at special times.

3 Playing cards can have numbers or pictures on them.

cardboard
Cardboard is very thick, strong paper.
Our cat sleeps in a cardboard box.

care (caring, cared)
1 If you care for something like a pet, you look after it.
You can have a kitten if you promise to care for it properly.
2 If you care about something, you think it matters.
She cares a lot about her paintings.

careful
If you are careful, you make sure you do things safely and well.
Be careful when you cross the road.

careless
Careless people do not think enough about what they are doing.
Peter is so careless – he's always losing things.

carpet (carpets)
A carpet is a thick cover for the floor.

carry (carrying, carried)
If you carry something, you take it from one place to another.
Will you help me carry this shopping?

carton (cartons)
A carton is made of thin cardboard or plastic. You can buy food or drink in cartons.
Can you get me a carton of milk?

cartoon (cartoons)

1 A cartoon is a film that uses drawings instead of actors.
There's a Bugs Bunny cartoon on today.
2 A cartoon is also a drawing that tells a joke.

case (cases)

You can keep or carry things in a case. There are cases to hold things like pencils or clothes.
I've packed my case already.

cash

Cash is money made of paper or metal.

castle (castles)

A castle is a large, strong building with very thick stone walls. Castles were built long ago to keep the people inside safe from their enemies.

cat (cats)

A cat is a furry animal. Small cats are often kept as pets. Large cats like lions and tigers live in the wild.

catch (catching, caught)

1 When you catch something, you get hold of something that is moving.
Our cat is good at catching mice.
2 To catch also means to get an illness that someone else has.
Mind you don't catch my cold.

caterpillar (caterpillars)

A caterpillar is a long, creeping creature that will turn into a butterfly or moth.

caught

See **catch**.
Elizabeth caught the ball in one hand.

cave (caves)

A cave is a big hole under the ground or inside a mountain.
The bear slept in a cave all winter.

ceiling (ceilings)

A ceiling is the surface above you in a room.
A balloon floated up to the ceiling.

cereal (cereals)

1 A cereal is a kind of grass grown by farmers for its seed.
Rice and wheat are cereals.
2 A cereal is also a kind of breakfast food.

wheat   rice   oats

19

a b Cc d e f g h i j k l m n o p q r s t u v w x y z

chain (chains)
A chain is a number of rings joined together in a line.

chair (chairs)
A chair is a seat with a back, for one person.

chalk (chalks)
1 Chalk is soft white rock.
The cliffs here are made of chalk.
2 Chalks are pieces of soft white rock that you write with.

change [1]
Change is the money you get back when you have given too much for something.
I haven't got the right money. Can you give me change?

change [2] (changing, changed)
When things change, they become different.
It was fun to watch the tadpoles slowly changing into frogs.

channel (channels)
1 A channel is a narrow ditch for water.
2 You have different channels on your television set. Each one has its own programme.

charge [1]
Someone who is in charge of something makes sure that it is looked after.
Mrs Dobson is in charge of the school library.

charge [2] (charging, charged)
When people charge you for something, they ask you to pay money for it.
The zoo charges for children to go in.

chase (chasing, chased)
When you chase somebody, you run after them and try to catch them.

cheap (cheaper, cheapest)
Something cheap does not cost very much.
I want the red shoes, but the blue ones are cheaper.

checkout (checkouts)
A checkout is a place in a shop where you pay for things.
We had to queue up at the checkout.

cheek (cheeks)
Your cheeks are the soft parts on each side of your face.
Debbie's cheeks were bright pink when she came in out of the snow.

cheese

Cheese is a food. There are lots of different kinds of cheese, but they are all made from milk.

chest (chests)

1 A chest is a big, strong box with a lid.

2 Your chest is the top part of your body, at the front.
Every time I cough, I get a nasty pain in my chest.

chick (chicks)

A chick is a baby bird.

Circus

chicken (chickens)

A chicken is a bird that farmers keep. Chickens lay the eggs that we eat.

child (children)

A child is a young boy or girl.

chin (chins)

Your chin is the part of your face that is under your mouth.

chip (chips)

A chip is a long, thin piece of fried potato.

chocolate (chocolates)

Chocolate is a sweet brown drink or food made from cocoa.

choose (choosing, chosen)

If you choose something, you make up your mind which one you want.
Why did you choose that shirt? The blue one was much nicer.

chose

See **choose**.
Luke chose a book on dinosaurs.

chosen

See **choose**.
Luke's sister asked why he had chosen a book on dinosaurs.

city (cities)

A city is a very big town.
London and New York are cities.

class (classes)

A class is a group of pupils who learn together.
Look, there's Sam. He's in my class at school.

a b **Cc** d e f g h i j k l m n o p q r s t u v w x y z

clean [1] (cleaner, cleanest)
Something that is clean has no dirty marks on it.
This floor is not very clean.

clean [2] (cleaning, cleaned)
When you clean something, you get all the dirt off.
I clean my teeth twice a day.

clear [1] (clearer, clearest)
1 If something is clear, it is easy to see, hear, or understand.
I found my way easily because the map was so clear.
2 If something is clear, it is free of things you do not want.
If the road is clear, you can cross.
3 If something like glass or plastic is clear, you can see through it.
The water is so clear, you can see the bottom of the pond.

clear [2] (clearing, cleared)
When you clear a place, you take things away.
The children cleared the lawn by raking up the leaves.

clever (cleverer, cleverest)
Someone who is clever can learn and understand things easily.

click (clicks)
A click is a short, sharp sound like the sound an electric light switch makes.

cliff (cliffs)
A cliff is a hill with one side that goes straight down. Most cliffs are near the sea.

climb (climbing, climbed)
When you climb, you go up or down something high.

cling (clinging, clung)
If you cling to someone, you hold on tightly.
The baby clung to his mother and would not let her go.

cloak (cloaks)
A cloak is a very loose coat without sleeves.

cloak

clock (clocks)
A clock is a machine that tells you what the time is.

22

close [1] (closer, closest)

When something is close, it is near.

In the fog, the children could only see things that were close to them.

---

close [2] (closing, closed)

When something closes, it shuts.

When Ben got to the shop, it was closed.

---

cloth (cloths)

1 Cloth is material for making things like clothes and curtains.

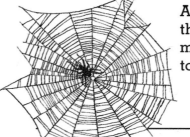

2 A cloth is a piece of cloth for cleaning or covering something.

---

clothes

Clothes are things like trousers and shirts that people wear.

---

cloud (clouds)

1 You can see clouds floating in the sky. They can be white or grey. Clouds are made of drops of water that sometimes fall as rain.

2 Clouds can also be made of dust, smoke, or steam.

Clouds of smoke rose from the bonfire.

---

coal

Coal is black rock that is burned to make heat.

coat (coats)

You put a coat on top of other clothes when you go out. Coats have long sleeves.

---

cobweb (cobwebs)

A cobweb is a thin, sticky net made by a spider to catch insects.

---

cocoa

Cocoa is a brown powder that is used to make chocolate, or a hot drink.

---

coin (coins)

A coin is a piece of metal money.

---

cold [1] (colder, coldest)

If you are cold, you feel that you want to put on warm clothes, or stand near something warm.

The weather got very cold and it began to snow.

---

cold [2] (colds)

A cold is an illness that makes you sneeze and your nose run.

---

collar (collars)

1 A collar is the part that goes round the neck of clothes like shirts and jackets.

My collar is too tight.

2 A collar is also a band that goes round the neck of a dog or cat.

23

a b c d e f g h i j k l m n o p q r s t u v w x y z

Cc

comfortable
If something is comfortable, it is pleasant to be in or to wear.
This chair is really comfortable.

comic (comics)
A comic is a paper with stories told in pictures.

computer (computers)
A computer is a machine that stores information. Computers can also work things out, or make other machines work.

control (controlling, controlled)
If you control something, you are in charge of it and can make it do what you want.
Please try and control that dog.

cook (cooking, cooked)
If someone cooks something, they get it ready to eat by heating it.

cooker (cookers)
A cooker is for heating food. It has an oven below for baking, and places on top for boiling or frying.

cool (cooler, coolest)
If something is cool, it feels quite cold.
I'm so hot. I'd love a cool drink.

copper
Copper is a red-brown metal used for making things like water pipes.

copy (copying, copied)
If you copy something, you do it exactly the same.
I want you all to copy the words I have written on the board.

corner (corners)
A corner is the point where two sides, edges, or streets meet.

cost (costing, cost)
If something costs a particular amount, that is how much you could buy it for.
How much did your bike cost?

cot (cots)
A cot is a bed for a young child. Cots have high sides to stop the child falling out.

cottage (cottages)

A cottage is a small house in the country or in a village.

cotton

1 Cotton is a light material made from threads of the cotton plant.
My shirt is made of cotton.
2 Cotton is also a thread for sewing.

cough (coughing, coughed)

When you cough, you make a sudden loud noise with your throat.
Smoke from the bonfire made us cough.

count (counting, counted)

1 When you count, you say numbers in order.
You count up to fifty, and I'll hide.
2 To count also means to use numbers to find out how many people or things there are in a place.
Count your change before you leave.

counter (counters)

1 A counter is a long table where you are served in a shop or bank.
2 A counter is also a small, round, flat piece of plastic used for playing games.

country (countries)

1 A country is a land with its own people and laws.
France, the United States of America, and China are all countries.
2 The country is land with farms and villages away from towns.

cover [1] (covering, covered)

If you cover something, you put another thing over it or round it.

cover [2] (covers)

A cover is something that goes over or around something else. Blankets are covers on a bed. Books also have covers.

cow (cows)

A cow is a large animal that gives milk.

crack (cracks)

1 A crack is a line on the surface of something where it has been partly broken.
There is a crack in this cup.
2 A crack is also the sharp noise that a dry twig makes when it breaks.

cracker (crackers)

1 A cracker is a thin biscuit.
2 A cracker is also a paper tube which bangs when two people pull it.
Our Christmas crackers had paper hats inside.

a b Cc d e f g h i j k l m n o p q r s t u v w x y z

25

a b Cc d e f g h i j k l m n o p q r s t u v w x y z

crane (cranes)
1 A crane is a machine that lifts very heavy things.

2 A crane is also a large bird with very long legs.

crash [1] (crashing, crashed)
When something crashes, it falls or hits something else with a loud noise.
The plates crashed to the floor.

crash [2] (crashes)
1 A crash is a very loud noise.
The lightning was followed by a crash of thunder.
2 A crash is also a traffic accident.

crawl (crawling, crawled)
When you crawl, you move on your hands and knees.
The baby can crawl now.

crayon (crayons)
A crayon is a coloured pencil often made of wax.

cream
Cream is the thick part on the top of milk, often used in cakes.

creature (creatures)
A creature is any animal.
A forest is full of strange creatures.

creep (creeping, crept)
1 An animal that creeps moves along close to the ground.
I saw a caterpillar creeping up a stem.
2 If you creep somewhere, you move quietly or secretly.
I saw you creeping out of the door!

crept
See **creep**.
We were late and crept in at the back.

crew (crews)
A crew is a group of people who work together, usually on a boat or aeroplane.

cricket [1]
Cricket is a ball game with eleven players on each side.

cricket [2] (crickets)
A cricket is a jumping insect that makes a shrill sound.

crisp [1] (crisper, crispest)
1 Things like biscuits that are crisp are dry and break easily.
2 Crisp fruit is firm and fresh.

crisp [2] (crisps)
A crisp is a very thin, dry slice of fried potato.
May I have a packet of crisps?

26

crocodile (crocodiles)
A crocodile is a large reptile that lives in rivers in some hot countries.

crop (crops)
A crop is a group of plants that are grown on a farm for food.

cross ¹ (crosser, crossest)
If you are cross, you feel annoyed about something.

cross ² (crosses)
A cross is a mark like this + or this x.

cross ³ (crossing, crossed)
If someone crosses something like a river or a road, they go from one side to the other.
Be careful when you cross the road.

crowd (crowds)
A crowd is lots of people in one place.
I lost my mother in the crowd.

crust (crusts)
A crust is the hard part on the outside of bread.

crust

cry ¹ (crying, cried)
When you cry, you let tears fall from your eyes.
My friend cried when she heard that her granny had died in hospital.

cry ² (cries)
A cry is a shout.
Tom heard a cry and ran to look.

cup (cups)
People drink things like tea from a cup. A cup has a handle.

curl ¹ (curls)
Curls are pieces of hair twisted into rings.

curl ² (curling, curled)
If you curl up, you sit or lie with your body bent round itself.

curtain (curtains)
A curtain is a piece of cloth that you pull across a window to cover it.

cut ¹ (cuts)
A cut is an opening in your skin made by something sharp.

cut ² (cutting, cut)
If you cut something, you use scissors or a knife.
May I cut a piece of cake for you?

a b **Cc** d e f g h i j k l m n o p q r s t u v w x y z

27

Dd

damage   (damaging, damaged)
If a person or thing damages
something, they spoil it in some way.
The storm damaged lots of trees.

dance   (dancing, danced)
When you dance, you
move about in time
to music.

danger   (dangers)
If there is danger, something bad
might happen.

dangerous
Something that is dangerous is likely
to kill or hurt you.
Crossing a busy road is dangerous.

dark   (darker, darkest)
1   If it is dark, there is no light.
We'll need a torch. It's dark outside.
2   If somebody has dark hair, it is
usually brown or black.

date   (dates)
1   A date is the day, the month, and
sometimes the year when something
happens.
Today's date is the 12th of June.
2   A date is also a
sticky, brown fruit that
grows on a palm tree.

day   (days)
1   A day is the twenty-four hours
between one midnight and the next.
2   The day is the time when it is light.
I've been working hard all day.

dead
If someone or something is dead, they
are no longer living.

deaf   (deafer, deafest)
Someone who is deaf cannot hear well.
Some deaf people cannot hear at all.

dear   (dearer, dearest)
1   Something that is dear costs a lot.
I'd like that but it's too dear.
2   Someone who is dear to you is a
person you love.

decide   (deciding, decided)
When you decide, you make up your
mind about something.
I can't decide which shirt to wear.

deck   (decks)
A deck is a floor on a ship or bus.

decorate   (decorating, decorated)
1   When you decorate something, you make it look pretty.
We decorated the tree with fairy lights.
2   When people decorate a room, they make it look fresh with paint or paper.

deep   (deeper, deepest)
Something that is deep goes a long way down from the top.
I'm not allowed in the deep end of the swimming pool.

deer
A deer is a large animal that can move very quickly. Male deer have big horns like branches on their heads.

defend   (defending, defended)
To defend means to keep someone or something safe from attack.
An octopus defends itself by sending out clouds of ink.

delicious
If something is delicious, it tastes or smells very nice.

deliver   (delivering, delivered)
If someone delivers something, they bring it to you.
The paper-boy delivers the papers every morning.

dentist   (dentists)
A dentist's job is to look after people's teeth.

describe   (describing, described)
If you describe someone or something, you say what they are like.

desert   (deserts)
A desert is very dry land where few plants can grow.

desk   (desks)
A desk is a kind of table where you can read and write.

diamond   (diamonds)
A diamond is a jewel that looks like clear glass.

dictionary   (dictionaries)
A dictionary is a book where you can find out what a word means and how to spell it.

die   (dying, died)
When someone or something dies, they stop living.
Plants die without water.

a b c **Dd** e f g h i j k l m n o p q r s t u v w x y z

29

a b c
Dd
e f g h i j k l m n o p q r s t u v w x y z

different

If something is different from something else, it is not like it in some way.
Our pens are different. Mine is red and yours is blue.

difficult

Difficult things are not easy to do.
This is a difficult tree to climb.

dig (digging, dug)

To dig means to move soil away to make a hole in the ground.
The dog dug a hole to bury his bone.

dinner (dinners)

Dinner is the main meal of the day.

dinosaur (dinosaurs)

A dinosaur is a large reptile that lived millions of years ago.
See **Dinosaurs** on page 123.

direction (directions)

1 A direction is the way you go to get somewhere.
The school is in that direction.
2 Directions are words or pictures that tell you what to do.
Read the directions on the bottle.

dirt

Dirt is dust or mud.
Wash that dirt off your knees.

dirty (dirtier, dirtiest)

Something that is dirty is covered with mud, food, or other marks.

My clothes always get dirty when I play football.

disappear (disappearing, disappeared)

If something disappears, you cannot see it any longer.
After two days, my spots disappeared.

disappointed

If someone is disappointed, they feel sad because something they were hoping for did not happen.
Jessica was disappointed when her best friend could not come to her party.

disaster (disasters)

A disaster is something very bad that happens suddenly.
The storm was a disaster. Thousands of trees were blown down.

discover (discovering, discovered)

When you discover something, you find out about it.
I've discovered a secret drawer.

discuss (discussing, discussed)

When people discuss things, they talk about them.
We discussed the best way to build the tree house.

30

dish (dishes)

1 A dish is for cooking or serving food.

2 The dishes are all the things that have to be washed up after a meal.

dishwasher (dishwashers)

A dishwasher is a machine that washes the dishes.

distance (distances)

The distance between two places is how far they are from each other.

The distance between my house and the bus stop is half a mile.

disturb (disturbing, disturbed)

If you disturb someone, you interrupt what they are doing.

Gran does not like to be disturbed when she is resting.

dive (diving, dived)

If you dive, you jump head first into water.

I can swim, but I can't dive yet.

divide (dividing, divided)

1 If you divide something, you make it into smaller pieces.

Divide the cake into six pieces.

2 When you divide numbers, you find out how many times one goes into another.

Six divided by two is three.

doctor (doctors)

A doctor is someone whose job is to help sick people get better.

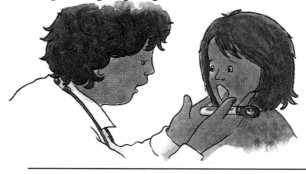

dog (dogs)

A dog is an animal that people keep as a pet or to do work. There are many different kinds of dogs.

doll (dolls)

A doll is a toy that looks like a small person.

donkey (donkeys)

A donkey is an animal that looks like a small horse with long ears.

a b c **Dd** e f g h i j k l m n o p q r s t u v w x y z

door (doors)
A door closes or opens the entrance to something like a house, a room, or a cupboard.
Will you hold the door open, please?

drag (dragging, dragged)
If you drag something, you pull it along the ground.

dragon (dragons)
A dragon is a monster with wings, that you read about in stories. Some dragons breathe out fire.

drain (drains)
A drain is a pipe that takes away water.
I pulled out the plug in the bath and the water went down the drain.

drank
See **drink**.
I was so thirsty I drank a glass of lemonade in one go.

draw (drawing, drawn)
When you draw, you make a picture with a pen, pencil, or crayon.

drawn
See **draw**.
I've drawn a dragon with my crayons.

dream (dreaming, dreamed or dreamt)
When you dream, you see and hear things in your sleep.
Last night I dreamed I saw a dragon.

dress ¹ (dresses)

A dress is something that girls and women wear. It is like a skirt and top in one.

dress ² (dressing, dressed)
When you dress, you put your clothes on.
You'd better dress quickly – you'll be late for school.

drew
See **draw**.
Ben found a piece of paper and drew an elephant.

drift (drifting, drifted)
If something drifts, it is carried gently along by water or air.
The boat drifted slowly into the bank.

drink (drinking, drunk)
When you drink, you swallow liquid.
Would you like something to drink?

drip (dripping, dripped)
When something drips, liquid falls from it in drops.
The tap in the bathroom is dripping.

drive (driving, driven)
When someone drives a car, a tractor, or a bus, they make it go where they want.
My uncle drives the school bus.

driven
See **drive**.
My sister has never driven on her own before.

drop ¹ (drops)
A drop is a tiny amount of liquid.
A drop of blood came from the cut on my knee.

drop ² (dropping, dropped)
If you drop something, you let it fall.
I dropped my glass and juice went everywhere.

drown (drowning, drowned)
If you drown, you die under water because you cannot breathe.

drum (drums)
A drum is a musical instrument that you beat with a stick.

drunk
See **drink**.
I have drunk my milk.

dry (drier, driest)
Something that is dry is not damp or wet.
Your socks are dry enough to put on.

duck (ducks)
A duck is a bird that lives near water.
Some ducks are wild and some live on farms.

dungeon (dungeons)
A dungeon is a prison underneath a castle.

dust
Dust is dry dirt like a powder.

duvet (duvets)
A duvet is a warm cover that you can use on a bed.

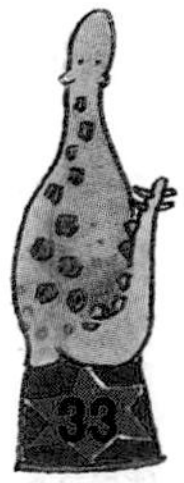

abcDdefghijklmnopqrstuvwxyz

33

abcd **Ee** fghijklmnopqrstuvwxyz

ear (ears)
Your ears are the part of your head that you use for hearing.

early (earlier, earliest)
1 Early means near the beginning of something.
She works best in the early part of the day.
2 If someone is early, they arrive before you expected them.
My uncle arrived early and waited until dinner was ready.

earn (earning, earned)
If you earn money you work for it.

earth

1 The Earth is the planet that we live on.
2 Earth is the material that plants grow in.
In the spring, the seeds in the earth begin to grow.

east
East is the direction of the rising sun.

easy (easier, easiest)
If something is easy, it can be done or understood without any trouble.
This book is really easy to read.

eat (eating, eaten)
When you eat, you take food into your body.
I'm hungry. When are we eating?

echo (echoes)
An echo is a sound that you hear again when it bounces back off something solid. You can often hear an echo in a cave.

edge (edges)
An edge is the part along the end or side of something.
Sam pushed his car across the table and it fell off the edge.

effect (effects)
An effect is anything that happens because of something else.
The cold weather had a terrible effect on the birds because the water froze.

effort
Effort is the hard work you put into something you are trying to do.
Make an effort to finish that today.

egg (eggs)
Baby birds, reptiles, amphibians, fish, and insects live inside eggs until they are big enough to be born. Birds' eggs are oval, with a thin hard shell.

elastic
Elastic is a strip of material that can be pulled to make it longer. When you let it go, it goes back to its usual size.
This elastic band is easy to stretch.

elbow (elbows)
Your elbow is the bony part in the middle of your arm, where it bends.

electricity
Electricity is power that moves along wires. It is used to give light and heat, and to make machines work.

elephant (elephants)
An elephant is a very big, grey animal with tusks and a very long nose, called a trunk.

empty (emptier, emptiest)
Something that is empty has nothing in it.
I wanted another biscuit, but the tin was empty.

end (ends)
The end is the last part of something.
I read the book right to the end.

enemy (enemies)
An enemy is a person who wants to hurt you.

energetic

Someone who is energetic is very active.

energy
If you have energy, you can be active and do things.
I had lots of energy this morning so I ran all the way to school.

a b c d **Ee** f g h i j k l m n o p q r s t u v w x y z

abcd **Ee** fghijklmnopqrstuvwxyz

engine   (engines)
An engine is a machine that uses fuel to make things move.
The driver started the engine and the bus moved off.

enjoy   (enjoying, enjoyed)
If you enjoy something, you like doing it.
I enjoy playing with my friends.

enormous
Something enormous is very big.

enough
If you have enough of something, you do not need any more.
Have you enough money to get the shopping?

enter   (entering, entered)
When you enter a place, you go in.
You can enter the school through the side gate.

entrance   (entrances)
The entrance to a place is the way in.

envelope   (envelopes)
An envelope is a paper cover for a letter.

environment   (environments)
Your environment is everything around you that has an effect on the way you live.
A healthy environment is important for everybody.

envy   (envying, envied)
If you envy someone, you want something they have.
I envy my cousins because their mum and dad are taking them camping.

equal   (equalling, equalled)
If something equals something else, the two things are the same size or the same number.
Two plus two equals four.

equipment
Equipment is the things you need for doing something.

escape   (escaping, escaped)
If a person or animal escapes, they get away from something.
My gerbils keep escaping. I shall have to get them a new cage.

estate   (estates)
1   An estate is an area of land with houses and sometimes flats on it.
My friend does not like the new estate because it is a long bus ride to town.
2   An estate can be a lot of land belonging to one person.

36

even

1 If a path is even, it is smooth.
2 If two scores are even, they are the same.
3 If numbers are even, they can be divided by two, with nothing left over.
Two, four, and six are even numbers.

evening (evenings)

The evening is the time at the end of the day before people go to bed.

excited

If you are excited, you are very happy about something and cannot rest.
I felt excited about the party.

excuse (excuses)

An excuse is what you say to explain why you have done something so that you will not get into trouble.
You're late again. What's the excuse this time?

exit (exits)

An exit is the way out of a place.

expect (expecting, expected)

If you expect something, you think it is very likely to happen.
We're expecting my uncle to arrive this evening.

explain (explaining, explained)

When someone explains something, they make it clear so that people will understand it.
Can you explain what makes a rainbow appear in the sky?

explode (exploding, exploded)

When something explodes, it blows up with a very loud bang.

explore (exploring, explored)

When you explore, you look carefully round a place for the first time.
As soon as the children arrived, they went out to explore the village.

extinct

If a kind of animal or plant is extinct, there are none living.
Dinosaurs have been extinct for millions of years.

extra

Extra means more than usual.
We'd better take extra jumpers in case it turns cold.

eye (eyes)

Your eyes are the part of your head that you use for seeing.

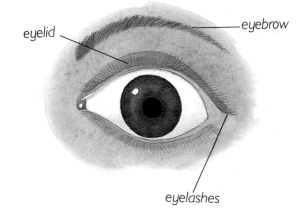

eyelid

eyebrow

eyelashes

a b c d **Ee** f g h i j k l m n o p q r s t u v w x y z

abcde Ff ghijklmnopqrstuvwxyz

face (faces)
Your face is the front part of your head.

factory (factories)
A factory is a building where machines are used to make things.

fail (failing, failed)
If someone fails, they cannot do something they have tried to do.
The pirates failed to find the treasure and had to leave without it.

fair ¹ (fairer, fairest)
1 Something that is fair seems right.
I was given a treat last week, so it is fair that my sister gets a treat soon.
2 Fair can mean light in colour.
My sister has long, fair hair.

fair ² (fairs)
Fairs are set up with stalls and roundabouts so that people can have fun.

fairy (fairies)
A fairy is one of the magic people you can read about in stories. Fairies usually have wings.

fall (falling, fallen)
When something falls, it comes down suddenly.
Don't fall out of that tree.

fallen
See **fall**.
I've just fallen over and hurt my knee.

family (families)
A family is made up of parents, children, and grandchildren.

famous
Famous people and things are very well known.
His aunt is a famous singer.

far (farther, farthest)
Something that is far is a long way away.
The next village is too far to walk to.

farm (farms)
A farm is a piece of land where people grow crops or keep animals for food.

fast (faster, fastest)
1 Something that is fast can move quickly.
I'm the fastest runner in the class.
2 If a clock or watch is fast, it shows a time that is later than the right time.
My watch is fast so I got up earlier than usual.

fat ¹ (fatter, fattest)
A person or animal that is fat has a very thick, round body.
That dog is much too fat. He needs to go for longer walks.

fat ² (fats)
Fat is something like butter or oil that can be used in cooking.

fault (faults)
If something bad is your fault, you made it happen.
It was Karen's fault that I spilt the tea – she made me laugh.

favourite
Your favourite is the one you like best.
This is my favourite toy.

fear (fears)
Fear is the feeling you get when you think something bad might happen to you.

feast (feasts)
A feast is a special meal for a lot of people.

feather (feathers)
A feather is one of the light things that cover a bird instead of hair or fur.

fed
See **feed**.
We fed the ducks on the pond.

feed (feeding, fed)
If someone feeds a person or animal, they give them food.
Will you feed the cat, please?

feel (feeling, felt)
1 If you feel something, you touch it to find out what it is like.
Just feel how soft this kitten is!
2 If you feel a particular way, like excited or tired, that is how you are at the time.
I feel sad now I'm leaving.

fell
See **fall**.
The apple almost hit me when it fell.

a b c d e **Ff** g h i j k l m n o p q r s t u v w x y z

felt
See **feel**.
After swimming ten lengths I felt very tired.

female (females)
A female is any person or animal that belongs to the sex that can have babies.

fence (fences)
A fence is a kind of wall made of wood or wire. People put fences around gardens and fields.

fence

field

fever (fevers)
When you have a fever, you feel very hot and ill.
The doctor told me to stay in bed because I had a fever.

field (fields)
A field is a piece of ground with a fence or hedge around it. Farmers grow crops or grass on fields.

fight (fighting, fought)
When people fight, they try to hurt each other.
The children were fighting with their feet as well as their fists.

fill (filling, filled)
If you have filled something, you cannot get any more in.
Richard filled his mug with milk.

film (films)

1 A film is a piece or roll of thin plastic that you put in a camera when you want to take photographs.

2 A film is also a story told in moving pictures.
There's a good film at the cinema.

fin (fins)
A fin is one of the thin, flat parts that stand out from a fish's body.
Fins help a fish to swim.

find (finding, found)
When you find something that has been lost, you get it back.
She found her book under the bed.

fine [1] (finer, finest)
1 Fine threads are very thin.
2 Fine weather is dry and sunny.

fine [2] (fines)
A fine is money that someone has to pay as a punishment.
I shall have to pay a fine if I don't take my book back to the library soon.

finger (fingers)
Your fingers are the five long, thin parts at the end of your hand.

finish (finishing, finished)
When you finish, you come to the end of something.
As soon as you have finished eating, you can go out to play.

fire (fires)

1 Fire is the heat and bright light that comes from things that are burning.
Wild animals are afraid of fire.

2 A fire is something that keeps people warm.

fire brigade (fire brigades)

A fire brigade is a group of people whose job is to put out fires.

firework (fireworks)

A firework is a paper tube filled with powder. When it is lit, it goes bang, or sends out small flashes of coloured light.

firm (firmer, firmest)

If something is firm, it is fixed so that it will not give way.
David tested the old bridge to make sure it was firm before he went across.

fish

A fish is an animal that lives and breathes under water. Fish are covered with scales, and they have fins and a tail for swimming.

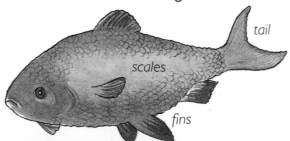

tail

scales

fins

fit¹ (fitting, fitted)

If something fits a person or thing, it is the right size and shape.
These shoes fit very well.

fit² (fitter, fittest)

Someone who is fit is healthy.
My mother keeps fit by walking to work.

fix (fixing, fixed)

1 To fix means to join something firmly to something else.
There was a shelf fixed to the wall.

2 If you fix something broken, you mend it.
Perhaps Dad can fix your aeroplane.

flame (flames)

A flame is one of the hot, bright strips of light that rise up from a fire.

flash (flashing, flashed)

When something flashes, it shines suddenly and brightly.
A flash of lightning lit up the sky.

flat¹ (flatter, flattest)

Something that is flat does not slope or have any bumps in it.
Find something flat to put your paper on.

flat² (flats)

A flat is a home. It is a set of rooms inside a house or a big building.
Gran's flat is on the ground floor.

flavour (flavours)

The flavour of something is what it tastes and smells like.
I like the flavour of pineapple.

a b c d e **Ff** g h i j k l m n o p q r s t u v w x y z

flew
See **fly**.
A bird flew low over the cat's head.

float (floating, floated)
1 If something floats, it stays on top of a liquid.

2 If something floats in the air, it drifts along gently.
A balloon floated above the rooftops.

floor (floors)
A floor is the part of a room or building that people walk on.
The children sat on the floor watching television.

flour
Flour is a powder made from wheat. It is used to make bread and cakes.

flow (flowing, flowed)
To flow means to move along like a river.
The stream flows very fast here.

flower (flowers)
A flower is the part of a plant that makes seeds. Many flowers are brightly coloured.

flown
See **fly**.
The birds have flown away.

fly ¹ (flying, flown)
1 When something flies, it moves through the air.
My aeroplane won't fly properly.
2 When people fly, they travel in an aircraft.
We are flying to Spain tomorrow.

fly ² (flies)

A fly is a small insect with one pair of wings.

food
Food is anything that you eat to help you grow and be healthy.

foot (feet)
Your feet are the parts of you that touch the ground when you are standing.

football (footballs)
1 Football is a game played by two teams who kick a ball and try to score goals.
2 A football is a large ball that players use in football games.

footprint (footprints)
A footprint is a mark left by a foot.

forehead (foreheads)
Your forehead is the part of your face above your eyebrows.

a b c d e **Ff** g h i j k l m n o p q r s t u v w x y z

foreign

Something that is foreign comes from another country.
We've got a foreign car.
It was made in Germany.

forest (forests)

A forest is a lot of trees growing together.
Wild animals live in the forest.

forgave

See **forgive**.
My friend broke my doll, but I forgave her because she didn't mean to do it.

forget (forgetting, forgotten)

If you forget something, you do not remember it.
Mum forgot where she put her purse.

forgive (forgiving, forgiven)

If you forgive someone, you stop being angry with them.
Please forgive me for losing my temper and shouting at you.

forgiven

See **forgive**.
I hope the teacher has forgiven me for behaving so badly yesterday.

forgot

See **forget**.
I forgot to take my sandwiches to school, so I was hungry all afternoon.

forgotten

See **forget**.
I know that boy but I've forgotten his name.

fork (forks)

A fork is a tool with three or four thin, pointed parts. People use small forks for eating and large forks for digging the garden.

fought

See **fight**.
The boys fought until both of them felt tired.

found

See **find**.
I've found my pen at last!

frame (frames)

A frame is something that fits round the edge of a picture or a window.

free (freer, freest)

1 If you are free, there is nothing to stop you doing something or going somewhere.
It was half term, so we were free to go and play on the swings.
2 Free things do not cost anything.
I got this badge free with my comic.

freeze (freezing, frozen)

1 When water freezes, it changes into ice.
2 People freeze food to stop it going bad.
3 If you say you are freezing, you mean you feel very cold.

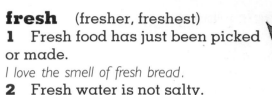

fresh   (fresher, freshest)
1   Fresh food has just been picked or made.
I love the smell of fresh bread.
2   Fresh water is not salty.
Many kinds of fish live only in fresh water, like lakes and rivers.
3   Fresh air is clean and pure.

fridge   (fridges)
See **refrigerator**.

friend   (friends)
A friend is someone you like and who likes you.

frighten   (frightening, frightened)
If something frightens a person or animal, it makes them feel afraid.
A car went by too fast and frightened the horse.

frog   (frogs)
A frog is a small animal with a smooth, wet skin. Frogs live near water.

front
The front of anything is the side that people usually see first.
We walked up the path and knocked at the front door.

froze
See **freeze**.
It was so cold that the pond froze.

frozen
See **freeze**.
Can you get me a packet of frozen peas?

fruit   (fruits)
Fruit is something like an apple or an orange which grows on a bush or tree. Fruits have seeds in them. See **Fruit** on page 120.

fry   (frying, fried)
When you fry something, you cook it in hot fat in a pan.

fuel
Fuel is something that can be burned to make heat or power. Coal, wood and oil can be used as fuel.

full   (fuller, fullest)
If something is full, there is no more room in it.

fun
When you have fun, you enjoy yourself and feel happy.

funny   (funnier, funniest)
1   Something funny seems strange.
There's a funny smell in here.
2   If something is funny, it makes you laugh.
This cartoon is very funny.

fur

Fur is the soft hair that covers some animals.

furniture
Furniture is all the big things like beds and tables that you need in a house.
Most furniture can be moved around.

a b c d e Ff g h i j k l m n o p q r s t u v w x y z

Gg

gale (gales)
A gale is a very strong wind.

game (games)
A game is something you play that has rules. Basketball and chess are games.

gap (gaps)
A gap is a space between two things.
The children squeezed through a gap in the hedge.

garage (garages)
1   A garage is a building where a car or bus is kept.
2   A garage is also a place that sells petrol or mends cars.

garden (gardens)
A garden is a piece of ground where people can grow flowers and vegetables. Someone's garden is usually next to their house.

gas (gases)
A gas is anything like air, that is not solid or a liquid. There are lots of different gases. Some gases have strong smells. Some gases burn easily and are used for heating and cooking.

gate (gates)
A gate is a kind of door in a wall, fence, or hedge.
The sheep got out through the gate.

gave
See **give**.
I gave Grandma a book for her birthday.

gentle (gentler, gentlest)
If you are gentle, you are quiet and kind.
Be very gentle with the kitten.

45

gerbil (gerbils)
A gerbil is a small animal with long back legs and very soft fur. Gerbils are often kept as pets.

ghost (ghosts)
A ghost is the spirit of a dead person that some people believe they have seen.

giant (giants)
A giant is one of the very big people in fairy stories.

giraffe (giraffes)
A giraffe is a very tall African animal with a long neck.

girl (girls)
A girl is a female child or young adult.

give (giving, given)
If you give something to someone, you let them have it.
What can I give Mum for her birthday?

given
See **give**.
I've already given you two biscuits.

glad (gladder, gladdest)
If you are glad, you are happy about something.
I'm glad you are coming to stay.

glass (glasses)
1 Glass is hard material that you can see through.

2 A glass is a kind of cup made of glass.

glasses
Glasses are a pair of glass lenses in a frame. People wear them in front of their eyes to help them see better.
My dad needs glasses when he reads or watches television.

glove (gloves)
A glove is a covering for the hand with places for the thumb and each finger.

glue
Glue is a thick liquid for sticking things together.

goal (goals)
1 A goal is the two posts that the ball must go between to score a point in games like football.
2 A goal is also a point that is scored when a ball goes into the goal.

gold
Gold is a valuable yellow metal.
My mum has a gold ring.

good (better, best)
1 Work that is good is well done.
2 If you are good, you behave well.
3 A good person is kind and caring.

grain (grains)
A grain of rice, wheat, or other cereal is a seed from the plant.

grass
Grass is a green plant with thin leaves. There are usually lots of these plants growing close together in fields or gardens.

greedy (greedier, greediest)
Someone who is greedy wants more than their fair share of money or food.

grew
See **grow**.
Our baby grew very fast at first.

ground
The ground is the earth or other surface that you walk on outside.
I dropped my sweet on the ground.

group (groups)
A group is a number of people or things that belong together in some way.
A group of children waited outside.

grow (growing, grown)
When somebody or something grows, they get bigger.

guess (guessing, guessed)
When you guess, you give the answer to something without really knowing it.
Can you guess what's in this box?

guitar (guitars)
A guitar is a musical instrument with strings.

abcdef **Gg** hijklmnopqrstuvwxyz

47

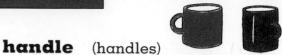

handle (handles)

Handles are put on things to make them easy to hold or carry. Cups, baskets, and saucepans have handles.

hang (hanging, hung)

When you hang something, you fix the top of it to a hook or nail.

hair

Hair is the soft covering that grows on the skin of people and animals.
My hair needs cutting.

hamster (hamsters)

A hamster is a small furry animal, with places inside its cheeks where it can hold food. Hamsters are often kept as pets.

hand (hands)

Your hands are the parts of your body that you use for holding things. A hand has four fingers and a thumb.
Wash your hands before you eat.

happy (happier, happiest)

When you are happy, you feel pleased about something, or like things the way they are.
She felt happy when her mum came home.

hard (harder, hardest)

1 Something that is hard is not soft.
The icing was so hard I nearly broke a tooth.
2 Things that are hard to do need a lot of effort.
Digging that hole was very hard work.

hate (hating, hated)

If you hate someone or something, you feel very strongly that you do not like them or it.
I hate getting up in the dark.

hay

Hay is dry grass that is used to feed animals.

48

head   (heads)
1   Your head is the part of your body that has your brain in it.
2   The head of something like a school is the person in charge.
Our school has a new head teacher.

---

health
Your health is how well or ill you are feeling.
My uncle worries about his health.

---

healthy   (healthier, healthiest)
1   If you are healthy, you feel well and full of energy.
What a lovely, healthy child!
2   Healthy things are good for you.
Brown bread is very healthy.

hear   (hearing, heard)
When you hear, you take sounds in through your ears.
Can you hear that dog barking?

---

heavy   (heavier, heaviest)
Things that are heavy are hard to lift or carry.

---

hedge   (hedges)
A hedge is a kind of wall made by bushes growing close together.

hedge

held
See **hold**.
Mum held my hand tightly.

helicopter   (helicopters)
A helicopter is a small aircraft without wings. It has blades that spin round on top. It can hover, or fly straight up into the air.

help   (helping, helped)
When you help somebody, you do something useful for them.
Can you help me carry the shopping?

---

hid
See **hide**.
I hid behind a tree so that my brother couldn't find me.

---

hidden
See **hide**.
Sophie has hidden my sweets and I can't find them.

---

hide   (hiding, hidden)
1   When you hide, you get into a place where you cannot be seen.
2   If you hide something, you put it into a secret place.

49

a b c d e f g **Hh** i j k l m n o p q r s t u v w x y z

high (higher, highest)
1 Something like a wall or a mountain that is high goes up a long way.
2 If something is high in the air, it is a long way up.
I threw a ball high into the air.

hill (hills)
A hill is land that is higher than the land around it.
You can see a long way from the top of a hill.

hit (hitting, hit)
If you hit something, you touch it hard.
I hit the ball so hard it went over the fence.

hive (hives)
A hive is a kind of box for keeping bees in.

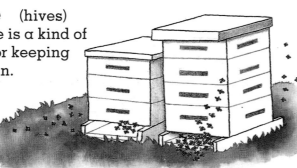

hold (holding, held)
1 If you hold something, you have it in your hands.
Hold the picture up so that we can all see it.
2 To hold means to have room inside for something.
This case will hold all my pencils.

hole (holes)
A hole is a gap or opening in something.
Dad dug a hole to plant the new tree.

holiday (holidays)
A holiday is time off from school or work.

hollow
Hollow things have an empty space inside.

home (homes)
A person's home is the place where they live.

honey
Honey is a sweet, sticky food made by bees.

hoof (hoofs)
A hoof is the hard part of a horse's foot. Cows and deer have hoofs, too.

hoof

hope (hoping, hoped)
When you hope that something is going to happen, you want it to, and think it is likely.
I'm hoping to get a bicycle this year.

horn (horns)

horn

A horn is a kind of pointed bone that grows out of the heads of cows and other animals.

50

horse   (horses)
A horse is an animal with hoofs that is used for riding and pulling carts.

hospital   (hospitals)
A hospital is a place where people who are ill or hurt are looked after.

hot   (hotter, hottest)
1   When something is hot, it burns if you touch it.
Don't touch the iron — it's hot.
2   If you feel hot, you are too warm.

house   (houses)
A house is a building made for people to live in.

hover   (hovering, hovered)
If something hovers, it stays in one place in the air.

human   (humans)
A human is a man, woman, or child.

hump   (humps)
A hump is a big lump on a camel's back.

hung
See **hang**.
Michael hung his coat on the hook.

hungry   (hungrier, hungriest)
If you are hungry, you want to eat something.

hunt   (hunting, hunted)
1   To hunt means to go after a wild animal to kill it.
Some animals hunt at night.
2   When you hunt for something, you look carefully for it.
I've hunted everywhere for my pen.

hurry   (hurrying, hurried)
When you hurry, you do something quickly.
I hurried to finish my breakfast.

hurt   (hurting, hurt)
When something hurts, you feel pain.
This scratch really hurts.

hutch   (hutches)
A hutch is a kind of cage for a pet rabbit.

a b c d e f g **Hh** i j k l m n o p q r s t u v w x y z

abcdefgh **Ii** jklmnopqrstuvwxyz

Ii

ice
Ice is water that has frozen hard.

ice cream (ice creams)
Ice cream is a sweet, frozen food.

idea (ideas)
An idea is something you have thought of.
I've got an idea for a good story.

ill
Someone who is ill does not have good health.

illness (illnesses)
Illness is bad health.
They closed the school because of illness.

imagine (imagining, imagined)
1 If you imagine something, you make a picture of it in your mind.
Imagine yourself in a dark wood.
2 If you can imagine something, you think it could happen.
I imagine Ben will win.

immediately
If you do something immediately, you do it at once.
Put those toys away immediately!

important
1 If someone is important, people take a lot of notice of what they say and do.
2 If something is important, it is very useful, or worth thinking about.
Listen carefully. This is important.

impossible
If something is impossible, it cannot be done.
It's impossible to jump over that high wall.

information
Information is facts that tell people about something.
I need information about museums in Oxford.

ink

Ink is the coloured liquid that is used for writing with a pen.

insect (insects)

An insect is a small creature with six legs. Flies, ants, butterflies, and bees are all insects.

instructions

Instructions are words or pictures that tell people what to do.

There are instructions for playing the game on the lid of the box.

instrument (instruments)

1 Instruments are things that help you do a job.

My dentist has lots of instruments.

2 An instrument is also something that you can use to make music.

A piano and a recorder are musical instruments.

interesting

If something is interesting, you want to spend time on it.

I'm reading a very interesting book.

interrupt (interrupting, interrupted)

If you interrupt somebody, you stop them saying or doing something for a short time.

Don't interrupt when I'm talking.

invisible

Things that are invisible cannot be seen.

Many living things are so tiny they are invisible without special instruments.

invite (inviting, invited)

If you invite someone, you ask them politely to come or to do something.

Are you inviting William to your party?

iron (irons)

1 Iron is a strong, heavy metal.

2 An iron is a flat piece of metal with a handle.

You make an iron hot and use it to make clothes smooth and flat.

island (islands)

An island is land with water all round it.

a b c d e f g h **Ii** j k l m n o p q r s t u v w x y z

abcdefghi

Jj

klmnopqrstuvwxyz

jam ¹ (jams)
1 Jam is fruit boiled with sugar until it is thick.
2 A jam is a lot of cars crowded together so that it is hard to move.
We've been stuck in a traffic jam.

jam ² (jamming, jammed)
If something jams, it becomes fixed and difficult to move.
This drawer has jammed and won't open.

jar (jars)
Jars are usually made of glass. They hold things like jam.

jelly (jellies)
Jelly is a sweet, slippery food that shakes when you move it.

jet (jets)
A jet is a very fast aeroplane.

jewel (jewels)
A jewel is a valuable and beautiful stone. Diamonds and rubies are jewels.

jigsaw (jigsaws)
A jigsaw is a puzzle. A picture is cut into pieces, and you have to put them together.

job (jobs)
1 Someone's job is the work that they do to earn money.
2 A job is also something you have to do.
My job is to take the dog for a walk.

joint (joints)
1 A joint is the place where two parts fit together. Your ankle is the joint between your foot and your leg.
2 A joint is a piece of meat.

joke (jokes)
A joke is something like a story that makes people laugh.

journey (journeys)
A journey is the travelling that people do to get from one place to another.
The journey takes two hours by bus.

jug (jugs)
A jug is used for holding and pouring liquids. It has a handle and a spout.

juice (juices)
Juice is the liquid in fruit.

jump (jumping, jumped)
When you jump, you go suddenly into the air.
I can't jump over that wall. It's too high.

54

kangaroo (kangaroos)
A kangaroo is a large, Australian animal that jumps. A female kangaroo has a pocket at the front, where it carries its baby.

keep (keeping, kept)
1 If you keep something, you have it as your own and do not give it away.
Do you want to keep your old teddy?
2 If you keep an animal, you look after it.
My father used to keep geese.
3 To keep also means to make something stay as it is.
Please try and keep your bedroom tidy.

kennel (kennels)

A kennel is a little house for a dog.

kept
See **keep**.
1 *I have kept all my old toys.*
2 *When I was small we kept hens.*
3 *I never kept my bedroom tidy.*

kettle (kettles)
A kettle is used to boil water in. It has a handle and a spout.

key (keys)
1 A key is a piece of metal shaped so that it fits into a lock.
2 A key is also a small lever that you press with your finger. Pianos and typewriters have keys.

kick (kicking, kicked)
When you kick, you hit something with your foot.

kill (killing, killed)
To kill means to make someone or something die.

kind ¹ (kinder, kindest)
Someone who is kind is ready to help other people.
It was very kind of you to get my shopping.

kind ² (kinds)
If two things are of the same kind, they belong to the same group.
A Labrador is a kind of dog.

king   (kings)
A king is a man who has been born to rule a country.

kiss   (kissing, kissed)
When you kiss someone, you touch them with your lips.

kitchen   (kitchens)
A kitchen is a room where food is cooked.

kite   (kites)
A kite is a light toy that flies in the wind at the end of a long piece of string.

kitten   (kittens)
A kitten is a very young cat.

knee   (knees)
Your knee is the bony part in the middle of your leg where it bends.

kneel   (kneeling, knelt)
When you kneel, you get down on your knees.

knelt
See **kneel**.
Steven knelt down to play with the cat.

knew
See **know**.
1   *I knew the answer to the sum.*
2   *I knew the man Dad was talking to.*

knife   (knives)
A knife is a tool with a long, sharp edge for cutting things.

knit   (knitting, knitted)
When people knit, they use wool and a pair of long needles to make clothes.

knock   (knocking, knocked)
When you knock something, you hit it hard.
My little sister knocked her head on the corner of the table.

knot   (knots)
A knot is the twisted part where something like string has been tied.

know   (knowing, known)
1   When you know something, you have found it out and you have it in your mind.
I know the answer to that question.
2   If you know somebody, you have met them before.
I know that boy. He lives in the next street.

known
See **know**.
1   *My brother has known how to play chess for two years.*
2   *I've known him for ages.*

label (labels)
A label tells you something about the thing that it is fixed on to. Labels on clothes tell you what they are made of, and how to clean them.

lace (laces)
1 Lace is material with a pattern of holes in it. It is often used to decorate things.
2 A lace is a piece of thin cord that is used to tie up a shoe.

ladder (ladders)
A ladder is two long bars with short bars between them. People use ladders for climbing up or down high places.

ladybird (ladybirds)

A ladybird is a small flying beetle. It can be red or yellow, with black spots.

lain
See **lie** ².
My jumper must have lain on the damp grass all night.

lake (lakes)
A lake is a lot of water with land all round it.

lamb (lambs)
A lamb is a young sheep.

lamp (lamps)
A lamp gives light where you want it.

land ¹
Land is all the dry parts of the earth's surface.

land ² (landing, landed)
When people land, they arrive by boat or aeroplane.

lane (lanes)
1 A lane is a narrow country road.
2 Wide roads are also divided up into strips called lanes.

language (languages)
Language is the words that people use to speak or write to each other.

a b c d e f g h i j k **Ll** m n o p q r s t u v w x y z

57

a b c d e f g h i j k L1 **m n o p q r s t u v w x y z**

lap [1] (laps)
Your lap is the part from the top of your legs to your knees, when you are sitting down.
Emma had a cat on her lap.

---

lap [2] (lapping, lapped)
When an animal laps, it drinks using its tongue.
Our kitten can lap milk now.

---

large (larger, largest)
If a thing is large, it is bigger than other things.

---

late (later, latest)
1 If you are late, you arrive after the proper time.
Sorry I'm late. I missed the bus.
2 Late can mean near the end of a period of time.
These flowers will come up in late spring.

---

laugh (laughing, laughed)
When you laugh, you make sounds that show you are happy or think something is very funny.

---

law (laws)
A law is a rule that everyone in a country must keep.

---

lawn (lawns)
A lawn is the part of a garden that is covered with short grass.

lay [1] (laying, laid)
1 To lay means to put something down carefully.
Please lay the flowers there.

2 When you lay a table, you get it ready for a meal.

3 When a bird lays an egg, the egg comes out of the bird's body.
Our hen laid an egg this morning.

---

lay [2]
See **lie** [2].
My brother lay on the bed, reading.

---

layer (layers)
A layer is something flat that lies over or under another surface.
There was a layer of snow on the path.

---

lazy (lazier, laziest)
Lazy people do not like working.
My sister is too lazy to tidy her room.

---

lead [1] (leading, led)
1 If you lead people, you go in front of them to show them where to go or what to do.
2 To lead also means to be in charge of a group.
William, you can lead this team.

---

lead [2] (leads)
A lead is a strap fixed to a dog's collar so that you can control it.

---

lead [3]
Lead is a soft, grey metal that is very heavy.

leader   (leaders)
A leader is a person or animal that is in charge of a group.

leaf   (leaves)
A leaf is one of the flat parts that grow on plants. Most leaves are green.

learn   (learning, learned or learnt)
When you learn, you get to know something you did not know before.
I've just learned how to knit.

leather
Leather is a strong material made from the skins of animals.
My shoes are made of leather.

leave   (leaving, left)
1   If you leave, you go away from somewhere or someone.
We shall leave home early tomorrow morning.
2   If you leave something somewhere, you let it stay where it is.
You can leave your bag here.

led
See **lead** ¹.
1   *A woman led us through all the rooms in the castle.*
2   *Sarah led our team on sports day.*

left ¹
Left is the side that is opposite to the right. In this picture, the cat is on the left.

left ²
See **leave**.
1   *We left home early in the morning.*
2   *I left my bag in the kitchen.*

leg   (legs)
1   Legs are the parts of the body that a person or animal uses for walking.
2   The legs of a piece of furniture are the parts that touch the floor.

lemon   (lemons)
A yellow fruit with a sour taste.

length   (lengths)
The length of something is how long it is. *Measure the length of this table.*

lens   (lenses)
A lens is a piece of glass or plastic that makes things look larger or smaller. Lenses are used in things like glasses and cameras.

lesson   (lessons)
A lesson is the time when someone is teaching you, or the things they teach you during that time.
My brother has piano lessons.

a b c d e f g h i j k **Ll** m n o p q r s t u v w x y z

59

a b c d e f g h i j k **Ll** **m n o p q r s t u v w x y z**

letter (letters)
1 A letter is one of the signs used for writing words. P, S, and E are letters.
2 A letter is also a message that you write to someone.

lever (levers)
A lever is a bar that is pulled down to lift or open something, or to make a machine work.

library (libraries)
A library is a place where a lot of books are kept for people to use.

lick (licking, licked)
When you lick something, you move your tongue over it.

lid (lids)
Things like boxes and jars have lids on top which open and shut.
Make sure you put the lid back on the biscuit tin.

lie ¹ (lies)
A lie is something you say that you know is not true.

lie ² (lying, lain)
If you lie, you rest with your body flat.

lifeboat (lifeboats)
A lifeboat is a boat that goes out to sea to save people's lives.

lift (lifting, lifted)
If you lift something, you move it upwards.
This bag is too heavy to lift.

light ¹ (lights)
Light is what lets you see. It comes from the sun, flames, and lamps.

light ² (lighting, lit)
If you light something, you start it burning.
Dad is going to light the fire.

light ³ (lighter, lightest)
1 Things that are light are easy to lift.
Feathers are very light.
2 Colours that are light are pale.
I have some light blue jeans.

lightning
Lightning is the bright light that flashes in the sky when there is a thunderstorm.

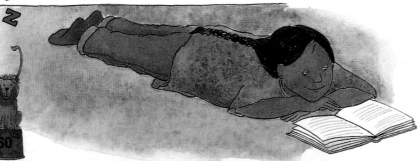

60

like¹

Something that is like something else is nearly the same.
Jill has got a cat like ours.

like² (liking, liked)

If you like somebody or something, you think they are nice.
I like apples.

likely

If something is likely, you expect it to happen.
Do you think it's likely to rain?

line (lines)

1 A line is a long, thin mark.
Write your name on the line.
2 A line is also a row of people or things.
There was a long line of people at the checkout.
3 A railway line is the set of metal rails that a train moves on.
A cow walked across the line and the train had to stop.

lion (lions)

A lion is a large wild cat that lives in Africa. A female lion is called a lioness.

lip (lips)

Your lips are the outside edges of your mouth.

liquid (liquids)

A liquid is anything that pours easily, like water, oil, or milk.

list (lists)

A list is a group of things or names that are written down one after the other.

eggs butter flour sugar

listen (listening, listened)

When you listen, you pay attention so that you will hear something.
I am only going to say this once, so listen carefully.

lit

See **light²**.
It was cold, so we lit the fire.

litter (litters)

1 Litter is paper, empty packets, bottles, and other rubbish dropped or left lying about.

2 A litter is all the young animals born to the same mother at the same time.
Our cat had a litter of five kittens.

little

1 If something is little, it is smaller than other things like it.
2 A little period of time does not last long.
This work will only take a little while.

a b c d e f g h i j k **Ll** m n o p q r s t u v w x y z

live   (living, lived)
1   If something is living, it is alive.
2   If you live in a place, that is where your home is.

load   (loads)
A load is a lot of something that is carried.
The lorry was carrying a load of rocks.

lock   (locks)
A lock is used to keep things like cases or doors shut. You cannot open a lock without a key.

long   (longer, longest)
1   Something that is long measures a lot from one end to the other.
An elephant has a long trunk.
2   Something that is long takes a lot of time.
Digging the garden is a long job.

look   (looking, looked)
1   When you look, you use your eyes.
Just look at that kitten!
2   If you look for something, you try and find it.
Can you help me look for my glasses?

loose   (looser, loosest)
If something is loose, it is not fixed firmly.
The bell on my bicycle is loose.

lorry   (lorries)
A lorry is a big, open truck for taking heavy things by road.

lose   (losing, lost)
1   If you lose something, you cannot find it.
I keep losing my keys.
2   If you lose in a game or a race, someone beats you.

lost [1]
See **lose**.
1   *I have lost my keys again.*
2   *We lost the game last Saturday.*

lost [2]
If someone is lost, they cannot find their way.

loud   (louder, loudest)
Something that is loud is easy to hear.

love   (loving, loved)
If you love someone, you like them very much.

low   (lower, lowest)
If something is low, the top of it is near the ground.
That wall is low enough to jump over.

lunch   (lunches)
Lunch is a meal that people eat in the middle of the day.

lying
See **lie** [2].
That dog has been lying there all day.

a b c d e f g h i j k **Ll** m n o p q r s t u v w x y z

62

a b c d e f g h i j k l **Mm** n o p q r s t u v w x y z

machine (machines)
A machine has parts that work together to do a job.
My mum made this dress on her machine.

made
See **make**.
1 *We made puppets in school today.*
2 *Now look what you've made me do!*

magazine (magazines)
A magazine is a kind of thin book that comes out every week or month. It has stories and pictures in it.

magic
In stories, people use magic to do impossible things.

magnet (magnets)
A magnet is a metal bar that can make pieces of iron or steel stick to it.

main
Main means the most important.
The main speaker tonight is the mayor.

make (making, made)
1 To make means to get something new by putting other things together.
I'd like to make a model aeroplane.
2 If you make a thing happen, it happens because of something you have said or done.
Blowing bubbles makes the baby laugh.

male (males)
A male is any person or animal that belongs to the sex that cannot have babies.

mammal (mammals)
A mammal is an animal that can feed its babies with its own milk. Dogs, people, and whales are mammals.

man (men)
A man is a fully grown male person.

manage (managing, managed)
If you can manage, you can do something although it is difficult.

map (maps)
A map is a drawing of part of the world. Maps tell you where different places are and show you things like roads, rivers, and mountains.

mark (marks)
A mark is something on a surface that spoils it.
How did you get that dirty mark on your shirt?

marmalade
Marmalade is a jam made from oranges or lemons.

marry (marrying, married)
When people marry, they become husband and wife.

mask (masks)
A mask is a cover that you can wear over your face.

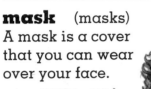

match [1] (matches)
1 A match is a small, thin stick that gives a flame when it is brushed on something rough.
2 A match is also a game played between two sides, like football.

match [2] (matching, matched)
If one thing matches another, it is like it in some way.

material (materials)
1 A material is anything that can be used to make something else. Wood and stone are materials.
2 Material is something that you can use to make things like clothes.

matter (mattered)
If something matters, it is important.
It doesn't matter what clothes you wear.

mattress (mattresses)

A mattress is the thick, soft part of a bed.

meadow (meadows)
A meadow is a field covered with grass.

meal (meals)
A meal is the food that you eat at one go at breakfast, lunch, dinner, tea, or supper.

mean [1] (meaner, meanest)
Someone who is mean does not like spending money or giving people things.

mean [2] (meaning, meant)
1 If someone asks what you mean, you tell them what you are trying to say.
I don't understand. What do you mean?
2 If you mean to do something, you plan to do it.
I'm sorry — I didn't mean to hurt you.

meant
See **mean** ².
1 *The teacher explained it carefully so that we knew what she meant.*
2 *I meant to tell you, but I forgot.*

measles
Measles is an illness that makes red spots come on your skin.

measure (measuring, measured)
When you measure something, you find out how big it is.

meat
Meat is a food. It comes from animals that have been killed.

medicine (medicines)
Medicine is liquid or pills that a sick person takes to help them get better.

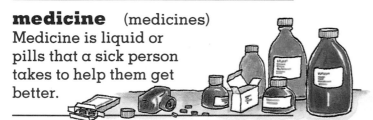

meet (meeting, met)
When people meet, they come together.
Let's meet in the playground later.

melt (melting, melted)
When something melts, it changes into a liquid.
My ice cream is melting.

mend (mending, mended)
When you mend something that is damaged, you make it useful again.
My brother can mend my bicycle.

message (messages)
You send a message when you want to tell someone something and you cannot speak to them yourself.

met
See **meet**.
I met Robin a few minutes ago.

metal (metals)
Metal is a hard material that melts when it is very hot.
Gold, silver, and iron are all kinds of metal.

mice
See **mouse**.

microwave (microwaves)
A microwave is a special oven that cooks food very quickly.

middle

The middle of something is the part that is the same distance from all its sides.

a b c d e f g h i j k l **Mm** n o p q r s t u v w x y z

65

midnight
Midnight is twelve o'clock at night.

milk
Milk is a white liquid that mothers and female mammals feed their babies with. People often drink cow's milk.

mind [1] (minds)
Your mind is the part of you that thinks, feels, understands, and remembers.

mind [2] (minding, minded)
1 If you mind about something, you are worried or made unhappy by it.
Gran doesn't mind being left alone.
2 If you mind something or somebody, you look after them for a short time.
Please mind the baby while I go to the shops.
3 If someone tells you to mind something, they want you to be careful.
Mind that broken glass.

mirror (mirrors)
A mirror is a piece of glass that you can see yourself in.

miss (missing, missed)
1 If you try to hit something and you miss, you do not hit it.
I tried to hit the ball, but missed.
2 If you miss somebody, you feel sad because they are not there.

mistake (mistakes)
A mistake is something that you did not get right.
I made two spelling mistakes. Mistacke

mix (mixing, mixed)
When you mix things, you stir or shake them until they become one thing.
Mix flour and water to make paste.

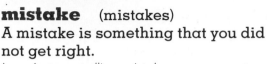

mixture (mixtures)
A mixture is made of different things mixed together.

model (models)
A model is a small copy of something.

moment (moments)
A moment is a very small amount of time.
Wait here – I'll only be a moment.

money
Money is the coins and special pieces of paper that people use to buy and sell things.

monkey (monkeys)
A monkey is an animal that lives in the trees in hot countries. It swings and climbs using its hands, feet, and long tail.

66

month (months)
A month is part of a year. There are twelve months in a year.

moon
The moon moves round the Earth once every twenty-eight days. You can often see the moon in the sky at night.

morning (mornings)
The morning is the time from the beginning of the day until twelve o'clock.

motorbike (motorbikes)
A motorbike is a kind of heavy bicycle with an engine.

motorway (motorways)
A motorway is a very wide road, made so that traffic can move fast.

mountain (mountains)
A mountain is a very high hill.

mouse (mice)
A mouse is a very small animal with a long tail and a pointed nose.

mouth (mouths)
Your mouth is the part of your face that opens for speaking and eating.

move (moving, moved)
1 If you move something, you take it from one place to another.
Move your toys before I tread on them.
2 If you move, you go from one place to another.
I'll have to move. I'm too hot here.

mud
Mud is wet earth.
We were covered in mud after playing football.

mug (mugs)
A mug is a large cup that does not need a saucer.

multiply (multiplying, multiplied)
When you multiply, you find the answer to a sum like this: 2 x 3 = .

muscle (muscles)
Muscles are the parts inside your body that help you move.

museum (museums)
A museum is a place where a lot of interesting things are kept for people to go and see.

mushroom (mushrooms)
A mushroom is a living thing that grows in the earth and looks like a little umbrella.

music
Music is the sounds that are made by someone singing, or playing a musical instrument.

a b c d e f g h i j k l **Mm** n o p q r s t u v w x y z

67

a b c d e f g h i j k l m **Nn** o p q r s t u v w x y z 1 8 4 6 68

nail (nails)

1 A nail is the hard part that covers the end of each finger and toe.
My nails are getting very long.

2 A nail is also a small piece of metal with a sharp point. Nails are used to join pieces of wood together.

name (names)

A name is what you call someone or something.
My friend's name is Rachel.

narrow (narrower, narrowest)

Something that is narrow does not measure very much from one side to the other.
The gap between the houses is very narrow.

nasty (nastier, nastiest)

1 Someone who is nasty is not at all kind.
She was so nasty she made her small brother cry.
2 Something that is nasty is not at all pleasant.

natural

Something that is natural has not been made by people or machines.
Wool is a natural material.

nature

1 Nature is everything in the world that has not been made by people.
2 A person or animal's nature is what they are really like.
Our cat has a lovely nature – she would never scratch anybody.

naughty (naughtier, naughtiest)

A naughty child is one who behaves badly.

near (nearer, nearest)

If something is near it is not far away.
Can I sit near the window?

nearly

Nearly means very close to something.
He's nearly tall enough to reach the shelf.

neck (necks)
Your neck is the part that joins your head to your shoulders.

---

need (needing, needed)
1 If people need something, they cannot live and be healthy without it.
Everybody needs water to drink.
2 If you need something, you cannot manage without it.
I need another sheet of paper to finish my story.

---

needle (needles)
1 A needle is a very thin, pointed piece of metal. Needles used for sewing have holes in them.
2 Needles can be thin rods used for knitting.
3 A needle can also be a thin leaf. Pine trees have needles.

---

nervous
1 If you are nervous, you feel afraid and excited because of something you have to do.
I felt nervous about being in the play.
2 A person or animal that is nervous is easily frightened.
Don't go near the nest – the mother bird is very nervous.

---

nest (nests)
A nest is a home made by birds, mice, and some other animals for their babies.

---

new (newer, newest)
1 Something that is new has just been bought or made.
I'm having a new bike for my birthday.
2 New can mean different.
I'm starting at a new school tomorrow.

news
News is information about what has just happened.
Have you heard the news? We won!

---

newspaper (newspapers)
A newspaper is a number of large sheets of paper folded together, with the news printed on them. Most newspapers come out every day.

nice (nicer, nicest)
If somebody or something is nice, you like them.
My new friend is very nice.

---

night (nights)

Night is the time when it is dark.

nightdress (nightdresses)
A nightdress is a kind of long, loose dress that women and girls wear in bed.

---

nightmare (nightmares)
A nightmare is a frightening dream.

a b c d e f g h i j k l m **Nn** o p q r s t u v w x y z

69

nod (nodding, nodded)
When you nod, you move your head down and then up again quickly, to show that you agree.

noise (noises)
Noise is a sound that someone or something makes.

noisy (noisier, noisiest)
A lot of loud sound is noisy.

nonsense
Nonsense is something that does not mean anything.
What a lot of nonsense she talks! The words do not make sense.

north
North is a direction. If you face towards the place where the sun comes up in the morning, north is on your left.
There is a city thirty miles north of here.

nose (noses)
Your nose is the part of your face that you use for breathing and smelling.

note (notes)
1 A note is a short letter.
Mum left a note telling us she would be late.
2 A note is also one sound in music.

notice [1] (noticing, noticed)
If you notice something, you see it and think about it.
I noticed the visitors next door.

notice [2] (notices)
A notice is a piece of paper or board that tells people something.

number (numbers)
Numbers tell you how many people or things there are. Numbers can be written as words (one, two, three), or as signs (1, 2, 3).

1066 999 21 071 50 nine Fifty 99 nine one 1 100 1992 nine 123 One Hundred

nurse (nurses)
A nurse is someone whose job is to look after people who are ill or hurt.

nut (nuts)
A nut is a kind of fruit that you can eat after you have taken off its hard shell.

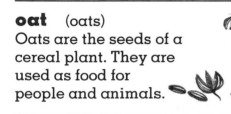

oar (oars)

An oar is a long pole with a flat part at one end. You need oars to row a boat.

oat (oats)

Oats are the seeds of a cereal plant. They are used as food for people and animals.

obey (obeying, obeyed)

When you obey, you do what someone tells you.

That dog always obeys his owner.

ocean (oceans)

An ocean is a very big sea.

The Pacific Ocean is the biggest ocean in the world.

octopus (octopuses)

An octopus is an animal with eight arms and a soft body. It lives in the sea.

odd (odder, oddest)

1 If something is odd, it seems strange.

That's odd! There was a cake on the table a minute ago and now it's gone.

2 An odd number cannot be divided by two without having something left over. 7, 13, and 27 are odd numbers.

3 Odd things do not belong to a pair.

offer (offering, offered)

1 If you offer something, you ask someone if they would like it.

Offer your friend a sweet.

2 If you offer to do something, you do not wait to be asked.

I offered to help wash up.

often

If something happens often, it happens a lot.

I often drop in to see my grandmother on Saturdays.

oil

Oil is a thick, slippery liquid. It can be burned to keep people warm, or put on machines to help them move easily. Some kinds of oil are used in cooking.

a b c d e f g h i j k l m n

o o

p q r s t u v w x y z

old (older, oldest)
1 Someone who is old was born a long time ago.
My grandfather is very old.
2 Something that is old was made a long time ago.
That picture is very old.
3 You say something is old if you have had it a long time.
My old shoes are not as nice as my new ones.

open
When things are open, people or things can go into them or through them.
Can you hold the door open, please?

opposite [1] (opposites)
The opposite of something is a thing that is as different from it as possible.
Tall is the opposite of short.

opposite [2]
If something is opposite something else, it is on the other side.
In the bus I sat opposite an old lady.

orange (oranges)
An orange is a round and sweet fruit with a thick peel.

orchestra (orchestras)
An orchestra is a large group of people playing musical instruments together.

order [1]
Order is the way something is arranged.
The letters of an alphabet are written in a special order.

order [2] (ordering, ordered)
1 If someone orders you to do something, they say you must do it.
The teacher ordered us to stop talking.
2 If you order something, you say that is what you want.
My mum ordered a salad sandwich.

ordinary
Ordinary things are not special in any way.
It was just an ordinary day.

oven (ovens)
An oven is the space inside a cooker where food can be baked.

owe (owing, owed)
If you owe money to someone, you have not yet paid them.
My dad owes me money for cleaning the car.

owl (owls)

An owl is a bird with large eyes. Owls hunt small animals at night.

own (owning, owned)
1 If you own something, it is yours.
2 If you own up, you say that you were the one who did something.

page (pages)
A page is one side of a piece of paper in a book.
Look! There's a picture on every page.

pain (pains)
Pain is the feeling you have when part of your body hurts.
I've got a nasty pain in my ear.

paint [1] (paints)
Paint is a liquid that you put on the surface of something to colour it.

paint [2] (painting, painted)
1 If you paint a picture, you make a coloured picture with paints.
2 If someone paints something like a door, they put paint on to it.

painting (paintings)
A painting is a picture that someone has painted.

pair (pairs)
1 A pair is two people, two animals, or things that belong together.

2 Things like trousers and scissors are also called a pair, because they have two parts joined together.
I've lost a pair of scissors.

palace (palaces)
A palace is a very large house where a king, queen, prince, princess, or bishop lives.

pale (paler, palest)
Something that is pale in colour is almost white.
When I was ill, I looked very pale.

palm (palms)
1 Your palm is the inside of your hand between your fingers and your wrist.

2 A palm is a tree that grows in hot countries. It has large leaves and no branches.

panic

Panic is sudden fear that you cannot control.

People saw the smoke and got into a panic.

---

pant (panting, panted)

When you pant, you take short, quick breaths.

Tom panted up the steep hill.

---

pantomime (pantomimes)

A pantomime is a kind of play. It tells a fairy story, and has songs and jokes in it.

---

paper (papers)

1 Paper is a very thin material that is used for things like making books, and for writing on and for wrapping things up.

This shop uses brown paper bags.

2 Paper is also short for newspaper.

The paper has lots of news today.

---

parcel (parcels)

A parcel is something that is wrapped up ready to be carried or posted.

---

park [1] (parks)

A park is a large garden where anyone can walk or play.

---

park [2] (parking, parked)

When people park a car, they leave it somewhere for a short time.

My dad parked the car near the flat.

part (parts)

A part is anything that belongs to something bigger.

One part of this puzzle is missing.

---

party (parties)

A party is a group of people enjoying themselves together.

---

pass (passing, passed)

1 If you pass something, you go by it.

I pass your school every day.

2 If you pass a test, you do well.

My sister has passed her driving test.

---

passenger (passengers)

A passenger is anyone travelling in a car, bus, train, ship, or aeroplane.

The passengers were cross because the train was late.

---

paste

Paste is a thick, wet mixture that you can use to stick paper to things.

---

pastry

Pastry is a mixture of flour, fat, and water which has been rolled flat and baked.

---

path (paths)

A path is a narrow way that you can go along.

There is a path up to the front door.

74

patient [1]
If you are patient, you can wait for a long time, or do something difficult, without getting angry.

patient [2] (patients)
A patient is someone who is ill and is being looked after by a doctor.

pattern (patterns)
A pattern is the way something is arranged, like lines and shapes on material, or sounds in music.

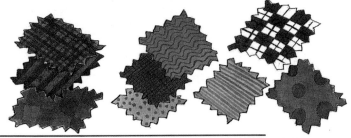

paw (paws)
A paw is an animal's foot.
The dog has hurt its paw.

pay (paying, paid)
To pay means to give money for work or for things that have been bought.

pedal (pedals)
A pedal is a part that you press with your foot to make something work. A bicycle has two pedals.

peel
Peel is the skin on some fruit and vegetables.
The peel on this orange is very thick.

pen (pens)
A pen is something you use to write with in ink.

pencil (pencils)
A pencil is a long, thin stick with black or a colour right through the middle. You use a pencil for writing or drawing.

people
People are men, women, and children.

perch (perching, perched)
When you perch on something, you sit on the edge of it, like a bird on a branch.

period (periods)
A period is a length of time.
The children were left alone for quite long periods.

person
A person is a man, woman, or child.

pest (pests)
A pest is any person, animal, or plant that is a lot of trouble.
Snails are a pest in the garden.

pet (pets)

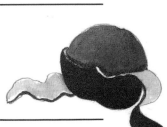

A pet is a tame animal that you keep in your home. Cats and dogs are pets.

a b c d e f g h i j k l m n o **pp** q r s t u v w x y z

75

phone (phones)
Phone is short for telephone.

photo (photos)
A photo is a picture taken with a camera. Photo is short for photograph.

piano (pianos)
A piano is a large musical instrument. It has black and white keys that you press down with your fingers.

pick (picking, picked)
1 If you pick somebody or something, you decide which one you want.
Pick three people for your team.
2 If you pick a thing up, you lift it.
Can you pick up that basket, please?
3 If you pick flowers or fruit, you take them from where they are growing.

picture (pictures)
A picture is a painting, drawing or photograph.

pie (pies)
A pie is meat or fruit covered with pastry.

piece (pieces)
A piece of something is part of it.
Can I have a piece of cake, please?

pier (piers)
A pier is a long, thin platform. It has one end on the land, and the rest goes out over the sea.

pig (pigs)
A pig is an animal that is kept on a farm.

pigeon (pigeons)
A pigeon is a bird with a fat body and small head.

pile (piles)
A pile is a number of things put on top of one another.

pill (pills)
A pill is a small, round piece of medicine which can be swallowed whole.

pillow (pillows)
A pillow is something soft that is made to rest your head on in bed.

76

pin (pins)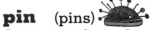
A pin is a short, thin piece of metal with a sharp point at one end and a flat head at the other. Pins hold pieces of paper or cloth together.

pipe (pipes)
A pipe is a long, thin tube that carries gas or water.

pipe

place (places)
A place is a particular part of a space or building.
Here's a good place for a picnic.

plain (plainer, plainest)
1 Something that is plain does not have a pattern on it.
Have you got a plain, blue material?
2 If something is plain, it is easy to see or understand.
The notice was quite plain.

plan (planning, planned)
When you plan something, you decide what is going to be done.
Mum and Dad are planning our holiday.

plane (planes)
Plane is short for aeroplane.

planet (planets)
A planet is any of the worlds in space that move around a star.
The Earth, Mars, and Saturn are some of the planets which go round the sun.

plant (plants)
A plant is anything that grows out of the ground. Trees, bushes, and flowers are all plants.

plaster (plasters)
1 A plaster is a sticky strip of special material for covering cuts.
2 Plaster is a soft mixture that goes hard when it dries. Plaster is used to cover the walls inside buildings.

plastic

Plastic is a light, strong material that is made in factories. It is used to make bottles, bowls, buckets, and many other things.

plate (plates)
A plate is a dish that you put food on.

platform (platforms)
1 A platform is part of a room that is higher than the rest.
The children went up to the platform to get their prizes.
2 A platform is also the place in a station where people wait for a train.

play (playing, played)
1 When you play, you do something for fun.
Why don't you play in the garden?
2 You can also play sports and games and try to win.
3 When musicians play, they make music.

a b c d e f g h i j k l m n o **Pp** q r s t u v w x y z

77

pleasant (pleasanter, pleasantest)
1 Pleasant people are nice to be with.
2 If something is pleasant, you enjoy it.
We had a pleasant walk with the dogs.

---

please (pleasing, pleased)
If somebody or something pleases you, they make you feel happy.
I was pleased to see my friend.

---

plenty
If there is plenty of something, there is more than you need.
Help yourself. There's plenty more.

plum (plums)
A plum is a juicy fruit with a stone in the middle.

---

pocket (pockets)
A pocket is a small bag which is sewn into clothes.
He always carries his pet mouse in his pocket.

---

poem (poems)
A poem is a piece of writing with a special rhythm. Poems usually have short lines.

---

point ¹ (points)
1 A point is the sharp end of things like pins and pencils.
2 A point is also part of the score in a game.
That's one point to me!

point ² (pointing, pointed)
When you point, you show where something is by holding out your finger towards it.

---

poisonous
Poisonous things would make you ill or kill you if you swallowed them.
Some berries are poisonous.

---

police
The police are people whose job is to see that no one breaks the law.

---

polite (politer, politest)
Someone who is polite is well behaved.
Ben is very polite. He always says 'please' and 'thank you'.

---

pond (ponds)
A pond is a small lake.

pony (ponies)
A pony is a small horse.

---

poor (poorer, poorest)
1 Someone who is poor has very little money.
2 Poor can also mean bad.
I can't see to read in this poor light.

---

porridge
Porridge is a hot breakfast food, made from oats boiled in water or milk.

possible
If something is possible, it can happen or it can be done.
It is possible to walk there in half an hour.

---

post [1] (posts)
1 A post is an upright pole fixed in the ground.
2 The post is the letters or parcels that are delivered to a home or office.
Is there anything in the post?

---

post [2] (posting, posted)
If you post something like a letter, you send it in the post.
I posted a card to Grandma yesterday.

---

pour (pouring, poured)
When you pour a liquid, you make it run out of something like a jug.

powder (powders)
Powder is something that is made up of very tiny pieces, like dust or flour.

---

power
The power of something is the strength that it has.
We need an engine with more power.

---

practise (practising, practised)
When you practise something, you keep doing it so that you get better at it.
I practise the piano every day.

present [1] (presents)
1 A present is something you give to someone.

2 The present is now.
Dad's not at home at present.

---

present [2]
Someone who is present is in a particular place.
The mayor was present at the opening of the new school.

---

president (presidents)
A president is someone who is chosen to rule a country.

---

press (pressing, pressed)
When you press something, you push hard on it.

pretend (pretending, pretended)
When you pretend, you act as though something is true when it is not.
I'll pretend to be ill, and you be the doctor.

---

prey
Prey is any animal hunted and eaten by another animal.
The eagle dived on to its prey.

---

price (prices)
The price of something is how much money you have to pay to buy it.

a b c d e f g h i j k l m n o **Pp** q r s t u v w x y z

79

a b c d e f g h i j k l m n o **Pp** q r s t u v w x y z

prick (pricking, pricked)
To prick means to make a tiny hole in something.
I pricked my finger on the needle.

prince (princes)
A prince is the son of a king or queen.

princess (princesses)
1 A princess is the daughter of a king or queen.
2 The wife of a prince is also called a princess.

prison (prisons)
A prison is a place where people are kept as a punishment when they have done something against the law.

prize (prizes)
A prize is something that people win.

problem (problems)
A problem is something that is hard to understand, to answer, or to deal with.
The problem with our puppy is it won't walk on a lead.

programme (programmes)
1 A programme is something like a show on radio or television.
2 A programme is also a list that tells an audience what is going to happen.

project (projects)
When you do a project, you find out as much as you can about something.
We're doing a project on dinosaurs.

promise (promising, promised)
When you promise, you say you will really do or not do something.
I promise I won't do it again.

proper
Proper means right.
I need the proper tool for this job.

proud (prouder, proudest)
If you feel proud, you are very pleased because you or someone close to you has done very well.
I was proud of my brother when he won.

pudding (puddings)
A pudding is something sweet like apple pie or trifle. You eat it at the end of dinner.

puddle (puddles)
A puddle is a small pool of water.

pull (pulling, pulled)
When you pull something, you get hold of it and make it come towards you.

puncture (punctures)
A puncture is a hole in a tyre.

punishment (punishments)
A punishment is something that is done to someone who has done wrong.

pupil (pupils)
1 A pupil is someone who is being taught something.
2 Your pupil is the black spot in the middle of your eye.

puppet (puppets)
A puppet is a kind of doll which can be made to move. Some puppets are like gloves, and you work them with your fingers. Others are moved with strings.

puppy (puppies)
A puppy is a very young dog.

pure (purer, purest)
Something that is pure does not have anything else mixed with it.
Pure orange juice has no sugar or water added to it.

purse (purses)
A purse is a small bag for holding money.

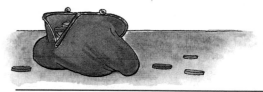

push (pushing, pushed)
When you push something, you use your hands to move it away from you.

puzzle (puzzles)
A puzzle is a game or a question that is hard to work out.
Do you like doing crossword puzzles?

P	U	P	P	E	T
U	P		I		I
D			P	I	G
D	O	G		E	
L		O		O	R
E	A	T	E	N	

pyjamas
Pyjamas are a pair of trousers and a jacket that you can wear in bed.

81

question (questions)
A question is something you ask when you want to find something out.

queue (queues)
A queue is a line of people waiting for something.
There was a long queue at the checkout.

quack (quacking, quacked)
When a duck quacks, it makes a noise through its beak.

quarrel (quarrelling, quarrelled)
When people quarrel, they talk angrily and sometimes fight.
My friend's mum and dad quarrel about spending money.

quarry (quarries)
1 A quarry is a place where people cut stone for buildings.

2 A quarry is also an animal or bird that is being hunted.

queen (queens)
1 A queen is a woman who was born to rule a country.
2 A king's wife is also called a queen.

quick (quicker, quickest)
1 Something quick is done in a short time.
I'll just have a quick drink.
2 To be quick means to move fast.
If you're quick, we'll catch the bus.

quiet (quieter, quietest)
If someone or something is quiet, they make very little noise, or no noise at all.
She was so quiet I forgot that she was in the room.

quite
1 If something is quite good, it is good but not special.
2 When something is quite ready, it is really ready.
The potatoes are not quite cooked yet.

quiz (quizzes)
A quiz is a kind of game. People try to answer a lot of questions to show how much they know.

rabbit (rabbits)
A rabbit is a small animal with long ears and a short, furry tail. Rabbits live in holes in the ground.

race (races)
A race is a way of finding out who is the fastest.
James won the swimming race today.

radiator (radiators)
A radiator is made of metal, and can be filled with hot water to heat a room.

radio (radios)
A radio is a machine that receives sounds through the air. You can listen to programmes or messages on a radio.

rail (rails)
1 A rail is a bar joined to posts to make something like a fence.
2 A rail is also a long metal bar that is part of a railway line.

railway (railways)
A railway is a set of rails for trains to run on.

rain
Rain is water that falls from the sky in drops.

rainbow (rainbows)
A rainbow is the band of different colours that you can see in the sky when the sun shines through rain.

ran
See **run**.
I ran hard to catch the bus.

rare (rarer, rarest)
Something that is rare is not often found, or does not often happen.
Some animals are becoming very rare.

a b c d e f g h i j k l m n o p q **Rr** s t u v w x y z

83

rat (rats)
A rat looks like a mouse, but is larger.

rather
1 Rather means a little bit.
It's rather cold today.
2 You say you would rather do something if you would like to do it more than something else.
I would rather watch the other channel.

raw
Raw food is not cooked.
You can eat raw carrots in a salad.

reach (reaching, reached)
1 To reach means to stretch out your hand to touch something.

2 To reach also means to arrive at a place.
We should reach London by teatime.

read (reading, read)
When you read, you can understand words that are written down.

ready
If you are ready, you can do something at once.
If you are ready, we can start the game.

real
Something that is real is not a copy.
This is a real diamond.

really
Really means you are telling the truth, or you want to hear the truth.
Are you really leaving this school?

reason (reasons)
A reason explains why you want to do something, or why something happens.
Is there a good reason why you don't want to be in the team?

receive (receiving, received)
To receive means to get something that has been given or sent to you.
I received your letter yesterday.

record [1] (records)
1 A record is a flat, round piece of plastic. It makes music or other sounds when it turns round on a record-player.
2 A record is also the best that has been done so far.
I got dressed in record time today.

record [2] (recording, recorded)
When you record something, you write it down or put it on tape or film.
Did you record that programme?

reflection (reflections)
A reflection is what you see in a mirror, or in anything shiny.

refrigerator (refrigerators)

A refrigerator is a metal cupboard that keeps food cold and fresh. It is often called a fridge for short.

refuse (refusing, refused)

If you refuse, you say you will not do something you have been asked to do.
Claire refused to help wash up.

remember (remembering, remembered)

To remember means to bring something back into your mind when you want to.
I can remember the names of everyone in my class.

Ann
Ben Claire
Jo Tilak
Susan Raj
William
Josh Yasmin
Mike Bob
Pippa

remind (reminding, reminded)

If you remind someone of something, you help them to remember it.

remove (removing, removed)

If you remove something, you take it away.
A rubber will remove pencil marks.

repair (repairing, repaired)

When someone repairs something, they mend it.
The men are repairing the road.

reply (replying, replied)

When you reply, you give an answer.
I'll reply to that letter tomorrow.

reptile (reptiles)

Reptiles are animals with cold blood. They have scaly skins, and short legs or no legs at all. Reptiles lay eggs. Snakes and crocodiles are reptiles.

rescue (rescuing, rescued)

If you rescue somebody, you save them from danger.
My mum dived into the river and rescued a little boy who couldn't swim.

rest ¹ (resting, rested)

When you rest, you lie down or sit quietly.

rest ²

The rest is the part that is left.
I've done most of my homework. I'll do the rest tomorrow.

a b c d e f g h i j k l m n o p q **Rr** s t u v w x y z

a b c d e f g h i j k l m n o p q **Rr** s t u v w x y z

result (results)
A result is anything that happens because of other things.
We were late, and as a result we missed the bus.

reward (rewards)
A reward is given to you for something good that you have done.
John was given a bag of crisps as a reward for clearing up the leaves.

rhinoceros (rhinoceroses)
A rhinoceros is a very large, heavy animal found in Africa and Asia. Rhinoceroses have horns on their noses.

rhyme (rhyming, rhymed)
Words that rhyme have the same sound at the end, like bat and cat.

rhythm (rhythms)
Rhythm is a repeated pattern of sounds in music and poetry.

rice
Rice is a white food that comes from the seeds of a kind of grass. Rice is the main food for many people.

rich (richer, richest)
People who are rich have a lot of money.

ridden
See **ride**.
Have you ridden your new bike yet?

ride (riding, ridden)
1 When you ride a bicycle or a horse, you sit on it as it goes along.
2 When you ride in something like a car or a train, you travel in it.

right ¹
If something is right, there are no mistakes in it.

right ²
Right is the side that is opposite to the left. In this picture, the dog is on the right.

ring (rings)
1 A ring is a circle.
There's a ring round the moon tonight.
2 A ring can be a circle of thin metal that people wear on their finger.
3 A ring is also the sound that a bell makes.

rise (rising, risen)
When something rises, it goes upwards. When the sun rises it appears above the horizon.

river (rivers)
A river is a lot of water that moves naturally and flows to the sea across the land.

road (roads)
A road is a way between places, made for cars and buses, bicycles, and trucks.

---

robot (robots)
A robot is a machine that can make some of the movements that a person can. In factories, robots can do jobs that people find boring.

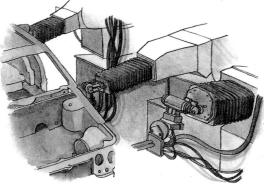

---

rock [1] (rocks)
Rock is the hard, stony part of the earth.

---

rock [2] (rocking, rocked)
If something rocks, it moves gently from side to side or backwards and forwards.
I hope the boat doesn't rock too much.

---

roll (rolls)
1 A roll of something like tape is a very long piece of it wrapped round and round lots of times.
2 A roll is also a small, round piece of bread made for one person.

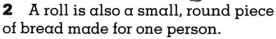

roof (roofs)
A roof is the part that covers the top of a building or vehicle.

---

room (rooms)
A room is one of the spaces with walls round it in a building. A room has its own door.

---

root (roots)
A root is the part of a plant that grows under the ground.

---

rope (ropes)
Rope is a lot of strong threads twisted together.

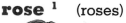

---

rose [1] (roses)

A rose is a flower with thorns on its stem. Roses often smell very nice.

---

rose [2]
See **rise**.
Black smoke rose from the bonfire.

---

rough (rougher, roughest)
1 Something that is rough is not smooth.
2 If people are rough, they are not gentle.

round [1] (rounder, roundest)
Round means shaped like a circle or a ball.

---

round [2]
Round means on all sides of something.
There was a fence round the field.

---

row [1] (rows)
A row is a line of people or things.

row [2] (rowing, rowed)
When you row, you use oars to make a boat move.

---

rubber (rubbers)
1 Rubber is strong material that stretches, bends, and bounces.
Rubber is used to make things like tyres.
2 A rubber is a small piece of rubber that is used to rub out pencil marks.

---

rubbish
Rubbish is things that are not wanted, like empty cans and waste paper.

ruby (rubies)
A ruby is a red jewel.

88

ruin (ruins)
A ruin is a building that is almost completely destroyed.

rule [1] (ruling, ruled)
1 Someone who rules is in charge of a country and the people who live there.
2 To rule also means to draw a straight line with a ruler.

---

rule [2] (rules)
Rules tell you what you can and cannot do. Games use rules, and places like schools have rules too.

---

ruler (rulers)
1 A ruler is someone who rules a country.
2 A ruler is also a strip of wood or plastic used for measuring and drawing straight lines.

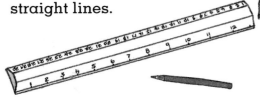

---

run (running, run)
When you run, you use your legs to move quickly.

sail ¹ (sails)
A sail is a large piece of strong cloth joined to a boat. The wind blows into the sail and makes the boat move.

sail ² (sailing, sailed)
To sail means to travel in a boat.
We sailed across the Atlantic.

salad (salads)
Salad is a mixture of vegetables eaten cold.

salt
Salt is a white powder you put on food to give it flavour.

same
If something is the same as something else, it is not different in any way.

sad (sadder, saddest)
If you are sad, you feel unhappy.
Katherine was sad at leaving her old school.

safe ¹ (safer, safest)
If someone is safe, they are free from danger.

safe ² (safes)
A safe is a strong box where money or valuable things can be kept.

sand
Sand is the powder made by tiny bits of rock that cover deserts and the land next to the sea.

sandwich (sandwiches)
A sandwich is two slices of bread and butter with a different food between them.

said
See **say**.
Simon said he was sorry.

Sorry

sang
See **sing**.
The children sang one song each.

a b c d e f g h i j k l m n o p q r **Ss** t u v w x y z

sank
See **sink**.
There was a hole in the boat and it sank.

sari (saris)
A sari is a long piece of cloth which many Asian girls and women wear.

sat
See **sit**.
We sat in front of the television.

saucepan (saucepans)
A saucepan is made of metal. It has a lid and a long handle. Saucepans are used to cook food.

saucer (saucers)
A saucer is a small plate for putting a cup on.

save (saving, saved)
1 If you save something, you keep it so that it can be used later.
I'm saving money for my holiday.
2 To save also means to free someone or something from danger.
A helicopter saved two men whose boat had sunk.

saw ¹ (saws)
A saw has a blade with sharp teeth on one edge. Saws are used for cutting material like wood.

saw ²
See **see**.
I saw my mother waiting outside.

say (saying, said)
When you say something, you use your voice to make words.
Did you say you were going out?

scale (scales)
A scale is one of the small, thin plates that cover the skin of fish and reptiles.

scales

Scales are used to find out how heavy things are.

school (schools)
School is the place where children go to learn.

scissors

A pair of scissors is a tool for cutting. It has two blades joined in the middle.

90

score [1] (scoring, scored)
To score means to get a goal or a point in a game.

___

score [2] (scores)
The score is the number of points or goals each side has in a game.

___

scratch (scratching, scratched)
1 If you scratch something, you damage it by moving something sharp over it.
Don't scratch the new table!

2 To scratch also means to move fingernails or claws over skin.
That cat has just scratched me!

___

screen (screens)
A screen is a smooth surface on which films or television programmes are shown.

___

sea (seas)
A sea is a very large area of salt water.

___

seal (seals)
A seal is a furry animal that lives in the sea and on land.

search (searching, searched)
When you search, you look very carefully for something.
I've searched everywhere for my watch but I can't find it.

___

season (seasons)
A season is one of the four parts of the year. The seasons are called spring, summer, autumn, and winter.

___

seat (seats)
A seat is anything that people sit on.

___

secret (secrets)
Secrets are things that must be kept hidden from other people.
We'll keep Mummy's birthday present a secret.

___

see (seeing, seen)
When you see, you use your eyes to get to know something.
Do you see that bird in the tree?

___

seed (seeds)

A seed is a tiny part of the fruit of a plant. Other plants of the same kind will grow from the seed when it is put in the ground.

___

seek (seeking, sought)
If you seek something, you try to find it.
They played 'hide and seek' all over the house.

___

seen
See **see**.
Have you seen my hamster anywhere?

a b c d e f g h i j k l m n o p q r **Ss** t u v w x y z

91

sell (selling, sold)
If someone sells you something, they let you have it for an amount of money.
The toyshop is selling a lot of things at half price today.

send (sending, sent)
If you send a person or thing, you make them go somewhere.
I'm sending a card to Grandpa.

sensible
Sensible people are good at knowing what is best to do.
It is sensible to wear warm clothes when it snows.

sent
See **send**.
Mum sent me to find you.

serve (serving, served)
If someone serves you in a place like a shop or a bank, they help you to get what it is you want.
Is anyone serving you?

set ¹ (sets)
A set is a group of things that belong together.
I would like a train set.

set ² (setting, set)
1 When something sets, it becomes solid or hard.
This jelly hasn't set yet.
2 When you set something somewhere, you put it there.
Set the plates on the table.

settee (settees)
A settee is a long, comfortable seat with a back, for more than one person.

sew (sewing, sewn)
To sew means to use a needle and cotton to join pieces of cloth together, or to fix things on to cloth.

sewn
See **sew**.

I've just sewn a badge on to my jacket.

sex (sexes)
The sexes are the two groups that all people and animals belong to. One group is male and the other is female.

shadow (shadows)
A shadow is the dark shape that is made by something blocking the light.

92

shake (shaking, shaken)
1 When a thing shakes, it moves quickly up and down or from side to side.
Everything shakes whenever a lorry goes by outside.
2 If you shake something, you make it shake.
Stop shaking the baby's cot.

shallow (shallower, shallowest)
Something like water that is shallow is not deep.
I can stand in the shallow end of the swimming-pool.

shape (shapes)
The shape of something is the pattern that its outside edges make.
A ball has a round shape.

share (sharing, shared)
If you share something, you make it into parts and give them to other people.
We shared the sweets between four people.

shark (sharks)
A shark is a large sea fish with sharp teeth.

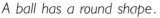

sharp (sharper, sharpest)
Things that are sharp have edges or points that can cut or make holes.
These scissors are not even sharp enough to cut paper.

shave (shaving, shaved)

When people shave, they cut hair from their skin to make it smooth.

shed (sheds)
A shed is a small wooden building. People often keep tools or bicycles in a shed.

sheep
Sheep are animals kept by farmers for their wool and meat.

sheet (sheets)
1 A sheet is one of the large pieces of cloth that people put on a bed.
2 A sheet is also a piece of material such as glass or paper.
This sheet of paper is big enough for my painting.

shelf (shelves)
A shelf is a long piece of wood fixed to a wall, for putting things on.

shell (shells)
A shell is the thin, hard part round eggs, nuts, and some kinds of animals such as snails.

a b c d e f g h i j k l m n o p q r **Ss** t u v w x y z

93

a b c d e f g h i j k l m n o p q r **Ss** t u v w x y z

shelter (shelters)
A shelter is a place that keeps people or animals out of the wind or rain.
There's a shelter at the bus stop.

shine (shining, shone)
When something shines, it gives out light, or looks very bright.

shiny (shinier, shiniest)
When things are shiny, they look very bright.
My dad has cleaned his car. It looks really shiny.

ship (ships)
A ship is a large boat that takes people or things across the sea.

shirt (shirts)
You wear a shirt on the top half of your body. Shirts have sleeves, a collar, and buttons down the front.

shiver (shivering, shivered)
When you shiver, you shake because you are cold or frightened.

shoe (shoes)
A shoe is a strong covering for the foot.

shone
See **shine**.
Dad cleaned his shoes till they shone.

shook
See **shake**.
I shook my money box, but there was nothing in it.

shop (shops)
A shop is a place where people go to buy things.

short (shorter, shortest)
1 A short time or distance is not very long.
It was a short walk to the shops.
2 A short person is not very tall.

shoulder (shoulders)
Your shoulder is the part of your body between the neck and the arm.

shout (shouting, shouted)
When you shout, you speak very loudly.
Alex shouted upstairs to his sister.

show [1] (showing, shown)
1 When you show something, you let it be seen.
Show me your new shoes.
2 If someone shows you how to do something, they do it so that you can watch them.
Can you show me how to mend a puncture?

show [2] (shows)
A show is something like dancing or a play, in a theatre or on television.
My uncle's taking us to a show tonight.

shower (showers)
1 A shower is a short fall of rain or snow.
We took shelter for five minutes while the shower lasted.
2 A shower in the bathroom gives you a spray of water so that you can stand under it and wash all over.

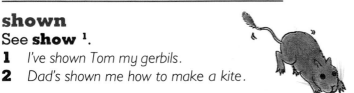

shown
See **show** [1].
1 *I've shown Tom my gerbils.*
2 *Dad's shown me how to make a kite.*

shut (shutting, shut)
To shut means to move a cover, lid or door to block up an opening.
Please shut the door. You're letting the cold in.

side (sides)
1 The side is the part that is on the left or right of something.
You start reading on the left side of the page.
2 A side can be an edge.
A triangle has three sides.
3 A side can also be a flat surface.
A cube has six sides.
4 The two sides in a game are the groups playing against each other.

sign [1] (signs)
A sign is anything that is written, drawn, or done to tell or show people something.

sign [2] (signing, signed)
When you sign, you write your name.
Fill in the form and sign it. Jane Dobson

silk
Silk is a very fine, shiny material. It is made from threads spun by an insect called a silkworm.

silver
Silver is a valuable, shiny white metal.

sing (singing, sung)
When you sing, you use your voice to make a tune.

a b c d e f g h i j k l m n o p q r **Ss** t u v w x y z

95

abcdefghijklmnopqr **Ss** tuvwxyz

sink ¹ (sinks)

A sink is a place where you do the washing-up.

sink ² (sinking, sunk)

If something sinks, it goes downwards, usually under water.

sit (sitting, sat)

When you sit, you rest on your bottom.
Children often sit on the floor instead of on chairs.

size (sizes)

The size of something is how big it is.

skeleton (skeletons)

A skeleton is all the bones that hold up the body of an animal or a person.

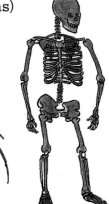

skin (skins)

1 Your skin is the outer covering of your body.
2 The outer covering of fruit and vegetables is also called a skin.

skirt (skirts)

A skirt is worn by women and girls. It hangs from the waist.

sky (skies)

The sky is the space above the Earth where you can see the sun, moon, and stars.

sleep (sleeping, slept)

When you sleep, you close your eyes and your body rests as it does every night.

sleeve (sleeves)

A sleeve is the part of something like a coat or shirt that covers your arm.
My sleeves are too long.

slept

See **sleep**.
I slept all night without waking up.

slip (slipping, slipped)

If you slip, you slide suddenly without meaning to.

slipper (slippers)

A slipper is a soft shoe that people wear indoors.

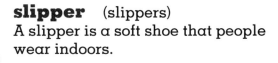

slippery

Something slippery is difficult to get hold of or walk on.
The soap was wet and slippery.

slope (slopes)
A slope is ground that is like the side of a hill.
The ball rolled away down the slope.

---

slow (slower, slowest)
1 Someone or something that is slow does not move very fast.
2 A clock that is slow shows a time that is earlier than the real time.
I'm sorry I'm late. My watch was slow.

---

small (smaller, smallest)
Small things are not as big as others of the same kind.
Fluff was the smallest kitten in the litter.

---

smash (smashing, smashed)
If something smashes, it breaks into pieces with a loud noise.

smell (smelling, smelt)
1 When you smell something, you use your nose to find out about it.
I can smell something burning.
2 When something smells, you can find out about it with your nose.
That rose smells nice.

---

smile (smiling, smiled)
When you smile, your face shows that you are feeling happy.

smoke
Smoke is blue or grey gas that floats up from a fire and looks like a cloud.

smooth (smoother, smoothest)
Something that is smooth does not have any lumps or rough parts.
The baby's skin is very smooth.

---

snail (snails)
A snail is a small creature that lives inside a shell. Snails are found on land and in water.

---

snake (snakes)
A snake is a reptile with a long body and no legs. Some snakes can give poisonous bites.

---

sneeze (sneezing, sneezed)
When you sneeze, you make a sudden noise as air rushes out of your nose.
I must have a cold – I can't stop sneezing.

a b c d e f g h i j k l m n o p q r **Ss** t u v w x y z

97

snow
Snow is small, white pieces of frozen water. It floats down from the sky when the weather is very cold.

soap
You use soap with water for washing. Soap can be solid, liquid, or a powder.

sock   (socks)
A sock is a soft covering for your foot and part of your leg.

soft   (softer, softest)
Things that are soft are not firm. Kittens' fur is soft.
The thick carpet was soft to walk on.

soil
Soil is the earth that plants grow in.

sold
See **sell**.
The man sold me this for half price.

solid
1   Something that is solid does not have air in it. A cricket ball is solid.
2   Something that is solid does not change its shape. Liquids and gases are not solid, but rocks and metals are.

song   (songs)
A song is words that are sung.

sore   (sorer, sorest)
Something that is sore feels painful.
I've got a sore throat and it hurts when I talk.

sort ¹   (sorts)
If things are of the same sort, they belong to the same group or kind.
What sort of cake would you like?

sort ²   (sorting, sorted)

When you sort, you arrange things into different groups.

sound   (sounds)
A sound is anything that can be heard.
I heard the sound of a dog barking.

soup
Soup is a liquid food made from vegetables or meat and water. You eat soup with a spoon out of a bowl.
We sometimes eat soup at the start of a meal.

sour

1   Things that are sour have the kind of taste that lemons have.
2   If milk is sour, it is not fresh.

south
South is a direction.
If you look towards the place where the sun comes up in the morning, south is on your right.

a b c d e f g h i j k l m n o p q r **Ss** t u v w x y z

98

space (spaces)
1 Space is the distance between things.
There's not much space between my bed and the wall.
2 In a building, the space is the part that is empty.
There's not much space in this room.
3 Space is everything beyond the Earth, where the stars and planets are.

spaceship (spaceships)
A spaceship is a machine that can carry people and things through space.

spade (spades)
A spade is a tool with a long handle and a short, wide blade. It is used for digging.

speak (speaking, spoken)
If you speak, you say something.

special
1 If something is special, it is better than the usual kind.
Mum made a special cake for the party.
2 Special also means made for a particular job.
You need special shoes for dancing.

speed (speeds)
Speed is how quickly something moves or happens.
Tortoises move at rather slow speeds.

spell ¹ (spelling, spelt or spelled)
When you spell a word, you name the letters in the right order.
H o r s e spells horse.

spell ² (spells)
In stories, a spell is a magic recipe or words that make things happen.
The witch said a spell that turned the wizard into a mouse.

spend (spending, spent)
1 When you spend money, you use it to pay for things.
2 When you spend time, you use it doing something.
We are going to spend Saturday at the zoo.

spent
See **spend**.
1 *I've spent all my money on sweets.*
2 *I spent an hour doing my homework.*

spider (spiders)

A spider is a small creature with eight legs. Many spiders make webs to catch insects.

spill (spilling, spilt or spilled)
If you spill a liquid, you let it flow out when you did not mean to.

a b c d e f g h i j k l m n o p q r **Ss** t u v w x y z

99

abcdefghijklmnopqr **Ss** tuvwxyz

spin (spinning, spun)
1 To spin means to turn round and round quickly.
When my bike fell over, the wheel went on spinning for a long time.
2 To spin also means to make thread by twisting long, thin pieces of wool or cotton together.

spine (spines)
1 Your spine is the row of bones down the middle of your back.
2 Spines are prickles or thorns on an animal or plant.

spire (spires)
A spire is a tall, pointed part of a church.
The church spire is so high you can see it above the other buildings.

spiteful
Someone who is spiteful says or does horrid things to upset people.
The witch was feeling spiteful and decided to turn the wizard into a toad.

spoil (spoiling, spoilt or spoiled)
If something is spoilt, it is not as good as it was before.
The rain spoilt my new shoes.

spoke
See **speak**.
The girl next door spoke to me today.

spoken
See **speak**.
Have you spoken to the new boy yet?

spoon (spoons)
You use a spoon to eat things like soup and pudding.

sport (sports)
A sport is a game or something else that is usually done outside. Football, running, and jumping are all sports.

spot (spots)
1 A spot is a round mark.
A leopard's coat has dark spots.
2 A spot is also a small, red bump on the skin.

3 A spot can mean a place.
Here's a good spot for a picnic.

spout (spouts)
A spout is part of something like a teapot or kettle. It is made so that you can pour liquid out easily.

spring (springs)
1 Spring is the part of the year when plants start to grow and the days get lighter and warmer.
2 A spring is a piece of metal that is wound into rings. It jumps back into shape after it has been pressed or stretched.

100

spun
See **spin**.
I spun round until I was dizzy.

stable (stables)
A stable is a shelter for horses.

stair (stairs)
A stair is one of a set of steps for going up or down inside a building.
Matthew went up the stairs to bed.

stand (standing, stood)
When you stand, you are on your feet without moving.
Don't just stand there – give me a hand.

star (stars)
1 A star is one of the tiny, bright lights you see in the sky at night.
2 A star is also somebody famous, like a singer or actor.

start (starting, started)
When you start, you take the first steps in doing something.
My sister is just starting to read.

station (stations)
1 A station is a place where people get on or off trains.
2 A station is also a building for the police or fire brigade.

steady (steadier, steadiest)
Something that is steady is not shaking at all.
Make sure the steps are steady before you climb up.

steam

Steam is very hot water that has turned into a cloud.

steel
Steel is a strong metal made from iron.

steep (steeper, steepest)
If a slope is steep, it is hard to climb.

stem (stems)

stem

1 A stem is the main part of a plant above the ground.
2 A stem can also be the thin part that holds a leaf, flower, or fruit on to the rest of the plant.

step (steps)
1 A step is the movement you make with your foot when you are walking, running, or dancing.
2 A step is also a flat place where you can put your foot when you are going up or down something.

a b c d e f g h i j k l m n o p q r **Ss** t u v w x y z

stick[1] (sticks)
1 A stick is a long, thin piece of wood.
2 A stick of anything is a long, thin piece of it.
Hand me that stick of chalk, please.

---

stick[2] (sticking, stuck)
1 If something sticks to something else, it becomes fixed to it.
My sweets are all sticking together.
2 If you stick something like a pin into a thing, you push the point in.

---

stiff (stiffer, stiffest)
Something that is stiff is not easily bent.
I need some stiff cardboard.

---

sting[1] (stings)
A sting is a sharp point with poison on it that some animals and plants have.

---

sting[2] (stinging, stung)
If something stings you, it hurts you with its sting.
A bee can sting you.

---

stir (stirring, stirred)
When you stir a liquid or a soft mixture, you move it round with something such as a spoon.

stone (stones)
1 A stone is a small piece of rock.
2 A stone is also the hard seed in the middle of some fruits such as cherries and plums.

---

stood
See **stand**.
I stood waiting for the door to open.

---

stop (stopping, stopped)
1 If a person or thing stops doing something, they do not do it for a time.
It has stopped raining so we can go out to play.
2 If something that is moving stops, it comes to rest.
The bus stopped to let the people off.

---

store (storing, stored)
If you store something, you keep it until it is needed.

---

storm (storms)
A storm is very strong wind with a lot of rain or snow.

---

story (stories)
A story tells you about something that has happened. Stories can be made up, or they can be about real things.

straight (straighter, straightest)
Something that is straight is like a line drawn with a ruler.
We could see a long, straight road in front of us.

---

straw (straws)
1 Straw is the dry stems of cereal plants.
2 A straw is a very thin tube for drinking through.

---

stream (streams)
A stream is a small river.

---

street (streets)
A street is a road with houses along each side.

---

strength
Strength is how strong someone or something is.

stretch (stretching, stretched)
When you stretch something, you pull it to make it longer, wider or tighter.
The skin on a drum is stretched tight.

---

strict (stricter, strictest)
When someone is strict, they make people do what they say.
The teacher is very strict so the class always works hard.

---

string
String is very thin rope.

---

strip (strips)
A strip is a long, thin piece of something.
A picture frame is made of strips of wood.

---

stripe (stripes)
A stripe is a thin band of colour.
Tigers have stripes on their bodies.

---

strong (stronger, strongest)
1 Strong people or animals are healthy and can do things that need a lot of energy.
2 Something strong is not easily broken.
We shall need a strong rope.
3 Food or drink that is strong has a lot of flavour.
I'd like a strong tea, please.

---

stuck
See **stick** ².
1 *The glue on my model hasn't stuck.*
2 *Tim stuck a pin in my balloon and it went bang.*

a b c d e f g h i j k l m n o p q r **Ss** t u v w x y z

103

abcdefghijklmnopqr **Ss** tuvwxyz

stung
See **sting** ².
I've just been stung by a bee.

---

submarine   (submarines)
A submarine is a boat that can travel under water as well as on the surface.

---

suck   (sucking, sucked)
If you suck something, you draw liquid from it into your mouth.

---

sudden
Things that are sudden happen quickly when you do not expect them.
There was a sudden crash of thunder.

---

sugar
Sugar is used to put in foods and drinks to make them taste sweet.

---

sum   (sums)
A sum is a problem that you work out using numbers.

---

summer   (summers)
Summer is the hottest part of the year.

sun
The sun gives the Earth heat and light. It is a star, and the Earth moves round it.

---

sung
See **sing**.
Our class has sung to the whole school.

---

sunk
See **sink** ².
My boat has sunk to the bottom of the pond.

---

sunny   (sunnier, sunniest)
It is a sunny day when the sun is shining.

---

supermarket   (supermarkets)
A supermarket is a big shop. People help themselves to things as they go round, and pay for them on the way out.

supper (suppers)
Supper is a meal eaten in the evening.

sure (surer, surest)
If you are sure about something, you know it is true or right.
I am sure that the shop is still open.

surface (surfaces)
The surface is the outer or top part of something.
Keep the surfaces in the kitchen clean.

surprise (surprises)
A surprise is something that you did not expect.
What a lovely surprise!

swam
See **swim**.
Today I swam for the first time.

sweep (sweeping, swept)
When you sweep, you use a broom to clear away dust and litter.

sweet (sweeter, sweetest)
Sweet things have the taste of sugar.

swept
See **sweep**.
Ben swept up all the leaves from the path.

swim (swimming, swum)
When you swim, you move your body through water without touching the ground.

swing (swinging, swung)

When something swings, it moves backwards and forwards from a fixed point.

switch (switches)
A switch is anything that you turn or press to start or stop something working.

swum
See **swim**.
Have you swum in the sea as well as the pool?

swung
See **swing**.
The door swung open.

syrup
Syrup is a sweet, thick liquid. Treacle is a kind of syrup.

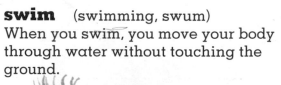

a b c d e f g h i j k l m n o p q r **Ss** t u v w x y z

table (tables)
A table is a piece of furniture. It has legs and a flat top.

tadpole (tadpoles)
Tadpoles are the babies of frogs, toads, and newts. Tadpoles live in water.
The tadpoles in the pond will turn into frogs.

tail (tails)
A tail is the part at the end of something. Most animals have tails, and so do aeroplanes.

talk (talking, talked)
When you talk, you speak to other people.
Most children start to talk before they are two.

tall (taller, tallest)
A tall person or thing measures more than usual from top to bottom.
There's a very tall tree in our garden.

tame (tamer, tamest)
Tame animals are not wild or dangerous. They can be kept as pets.

tap (taps)

A tap controls the flow of liquid or gas. There are taps in the bathroom to turn water on and off.

tape (tapes)
1 A tape is a special strip of plastic used to record sound or pictures.
2 Some tape has a sticky back. You can use it to hold paper together.

taste [1]
The taste of something is the flavour that it has.

taste [2] (tasting, tasted)
When you taste something, you eat or drink a little of it to see what it is like.

106

taught
See **teach**.
My brother has been taught to swim.

tea
1 Tea is a hot drink, made with boiling water and the dried leaves of tea plants.

2 Tea is also a meal that people have in the afternoon or evening.

teach (teaching, taught)
When someone teaches, they help people to understand something, or show them how to do it.
My aunt teaches swimming.

teacher (teachers)
A teacher is someone whose job is to teach.

team (teams)
A team is a group of people who work together, or who play together on the same side.
Our team won last Saturday.

teeth
See **tooth**.

telephone (telephones)
You can use a telephone to speak to someone far away.

television (televisions)
A television is a machine that receives sounds and pictures through the air.
We watched a tennis match on television yesterday.

tell (telling, told)
If somebody tells you something, they pass on news, a story, or instructions.
Instructions tell you what to do.

tent (tents)
A tent is a shelter made of canvas stretched over poles. Some people live in tents when they are on holiday.

term (terms)
A term is part of a school year. It is the time in between the main holidays, when the school is open.

theatre (theatres)
A theatre is a place where people go to see plays and shows.

thick (thicker, thickest)
1 Something that is thick measures a lot from one side to the other.
I'd like a thicker slice of cake.
2 Thick liquids do not flow easily.

a b c d e f g h i j k l m n o p q r s **Tt** u v w x y z

thin (thinner, thinnest)
1 A thin person or animal does not weigh very much.
2 Something that is thin does not measure much from one side to the other.
Thin paper tears easily.

thirsty (thirstier, thirstiest)
If you are thirsty,
you want a drink.

thread (threads)
Thread is a long, thin piece of something like cotton or wool.

threw
See **throw**.
Julia threw a stone into the pond.

throat (throats)
Your throat is the front part of your neck, and the tubes inside that take food, drink, and air into your body.

throw (throwing, thrown)
When you throw something, you make it leave your hand and move through the air.

thrown
See **throw**.
I've thrown my ball over the wall.

thumb (thumbs)
Your thumb is the short, thick finger at the side of your hand.

thunder
Thunder is the loud noise that follows a flash of lightning in a storm.

thunderstorm (thunderstorms)
A storm with thunder and lightning.

tie ¹ (ties)
1 A tie is a long strip of material that goes round the collar of a shirt and hangs down the front.
2 When two people do as well as each other in a race, it is called a tie.

tie ² (tying, tied)
When you tie something, you make a knot.

tiger (tigers)
A tiger is a big wild cat found in India and China. It has yellow fur with black stripes.

time
1 Time is measured in minutes, hours, days, and years.
2 The time is a particular moment in the day.
It's seven o'clock — time to get up!

Tt

108

tin (tins)
1 Tin is a silvery metal.
2 A tin is something that keeps food fresh.

---

tiny (tinier, tiniest)
Tiny things are very small.

---

toe (toes)
Your toe is one of the five parts at the end of your foot.

---

told
See **tell**.
I've already told you once.

---

tongue (tongues)
Your tongue is the long, soft, pink part that moves about inside your mouth.

---

tool (tools)
A tool is something that you use to help you do a job. Hammers and saws are tools.

---

tooth (teeth)
A tooth is one of the hard, white parts in your mouth.

---

top (tops)
1 The top of something is the highest part.
We climbed to the top of the hill.
2 The top is the part that covers something like a jar or tube.
Put the top back on your pen.

touch (touching, touched)
1 If you touch something, you feel it with part of your body.
2 If things are touching, they are so close there is no space between them.

---

town (towns)
A town is a place with a lot of houses, shops and other buildings.

---

toy (toys)
A toy is something you play with.

---

traffic
Traffic is cars, buses, lorries, and other things travelling on the road.

---

train [1] (trains)
A train carries people or things on railway lines.

---

train [2] (training, trained)
To train means to teach a person or animal how to do something.
I'm training my dog to walk on a lead.

---

travel (travelling, travelled)
When you travel, you make a journey.
I travel to school by bus.

a b c d e f g h i j k l m n o p q r s **Tt** u v w x y z

tree   (trees)
A tree is any tall plant with leaves, branches, and a thick stem of wood.

trousers
Trousers cover each leg and the lower part of your body.

truck   (trucks)
1   A truck is a kind of lorry.
2   Trucks are also carts pulled by a railway engine. Trucks are used for carrying things like coal.

true   (truer, truest)
1   Something that is true is right.
It is true that the sun is hot?
2   If a story is true, it really happened.

trunk   (trunks)
1   A trunk is the thick, woody stem of a tree.
2   An elephant's trunk is its long nose.
3   A trunk is also a large box for storing things or carrying things on a journey.

tube   (tubes)
1   Tubes are used to hold soft mixtures such as toothpaste.

2   A tube is also a kind of pipe.

tunnel   (tunnels)
A tunnel is a long hole under the ground or through a hill.

turn [1]   (turning, turned)
1   When you turn, you move round.
Please turn and face this way.
2   When something turns into something else, it changes.

turn [2]   (turns)
If it is your turn, it is time for you to do something.
It's my turn to ride the bicycle.

tusk   (tusks)
A tusk is one of the two long, pointed teeth that elephants have.

twist   (twisting, twisted)
1   When you twist something, you turn or bend it.
My mum twisted her ankle.
2   To twist also means to wrap things round each other.
Rope is made by twisting threads.

typewriter   (typewriters)
A typewriter is a machine with keys that you press to print letters and numbers.

tyre   (tyres)
A tyre is a circle of rubber fitted round the edge of a wheel.

ugly (uglier, ugliest)
People and things that are ugly are not pleasant to look at.

umbrella (umbrellas)
An umbrella is cloth stretched over a frame, which you can hold over your head to keep off the rain.

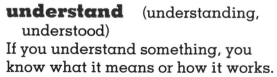

understand (understanding, understood)
If you understand something, you know what it means or how it works.

understood
See **understand**.
The class understood how to do the sum.

uniform (uniforms)
A uniform is a special set of clothes for people who belong to a group.

upright
Something upright stands straight up.
A post stands upright in the ground.

upset
When you are upset, you feel unhappy and sad.
My mum gets upset when we are naughty.

upside down
When something is upside down, the bottom part is at the top.
I held my bag upside down and everything fell out.

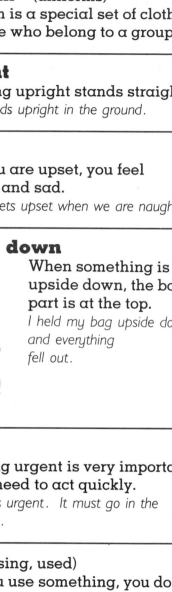

urgent
Something urgent is very important and you need to act quickly.
This letter is urgent. It must go in the post tonight.

use (using, used)
When you use something, you do a job with it.
You'll have to use a screwdriver.

useful
Something that is useful can be used to help you in some way.

usual
Something that is usual is what happens most times.
We'll have dinner at the usual time.

a b c d e f g h i j k l m n o p q r s t **Uu** v w x y z

a b c d e f g h i j k l m n o p q r s t u **Vv** w x y z

vehicle (vehicles)
A vehicle is anything that takes people and things from place to place on land. Cars, trucks, and bicycles are vehicles.

valley (valleys)
A valley is low land between hills.

valuable
Valuable things are worth a lot of money.
These rings are very valuable.

van (vans)
A van is a covered vehicle for carrying things and people.

vegetable (vegetables)
A vegetable is part of a plant that is used as food. Carrots, cabbage, peas, potatoes, and beans are all vegetables.

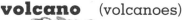

video (videos)
1 A video is sound and pictures recorded on special tape, to be shown on a television set.
2 A video is also a machine that can be used to play video tapes on a television set.

village (villages)
A village is a group of houses together with other buildings in the country.

voice (voices)
Your voice is the sound you make when you are speaking or singing.

volcano (volcanoes)
A volcano is a mountain that sometimes has hot liquid, gases, and ash bursting out of it.

wait (waiting, waited)
If you wait, you stay for something that you are expecting to happen.
We stood waiting for the bus to come.

walk (walking, walked)
When you walk, you move along on foot.

wall (walls)
1 A wall is any one of the sides of a building or room.
2 Walls made of brick or stone are also used round fields and gardens.

wand (wands)
A wand is a thin stick. In stories, fairies and wizards have wands. They use them for magic.

want (wanting, wanted)
When you want something, you need it, or you would like to have it.
I want some new shoes for school.

warm (warmer, warmest)
If you are warm, you feel somewhere between cool and hot.

warn (warning, warned)
If you warn someone, you tell them that there is danger.
Dad warned us not to go near the river.

wash (washing, washed)

When you wash, you make something clean with water and soap.

wasp (wasps)

A wasp is an insect with wings. It has a sting.

waste ¹
Waste is things that are to be thrown away, usually because the useful part has been removed.
Put tins, rubbish, and other waste in the dustbin.

waste ² (wasting, wasted)
If you waste something, you use more of it than you need to.
She wastes water by leaving the tap running.

a b c d e f g h i j k l m n o p q r s t u v **Ww** x y z

watch [1] (watching, watched)
If you watch something, you look to see what happens.
You're watching too much television.

watch [2] (watches)
A watch is a small clock that you can wear.

water
Water is the liquid in rivers and seas. It falls from the sky as rain.

wax
Wax is used to make candles and polish. It is soft and melts easily. Some wax is made by bees, and some is made from oil.

weak (weaker, weakest)
People or things that are weak are not strong.
She was so weak that she could not stand up.

wear (wearing, worn)
1 When you wear something, you are dressed in it.
I shall wear my new trousers for the party.
2 If something wears out, it becomes weak and useless because it has been used so much.

weather
The weather is how it is outside, for example sunny or raining.

week (weeks)
A week is seven days.

weigh (weighing, weighed)
When you weigh something, you find out how heavy it is.

well [1] (better, best)
If you are well, you are healthy.

well [2]
If you do something well, you are good at it, or make a good job of it.
My teacher says I write well.

west
West is the direction you look in to see the sun go down in the evening.

wet (wetter, wettest)
If something is wet, it is covered in water, or it has water in it.

whale (whales)
A whale is a very large sea animal. It breathes through a hole in the top of its head.

wheat
Wheat is a plant grown by farmers. Its seed is used for making flour.

whisper   (whispering, whispered)
When you whisper, you speak
very softly.

---

whistle ¹
When you whistle you make a loud,
high sound by blowing air through
your lips.

---

whistle ²   (whistles)
A whistle is a small tube that makes
a loud, high
sound when
you blow it.

---

wide   (wider, widest)
Something that is wide measures a
lot from side to side.
The stream is too wide to jump across.

---

wild   (wilder, wildest)
Animals and plants that are wild are
not looked after by people.

---

win   (winning, won)
When you win, you beat everybody
else in a game or race.

---

wind   (winds)
A wind is air moving along quickly.
The wind blew the leaves everywhere.

---

window   (windows)
A window is an opening in the wall of
a building, or in a vehicle.

---

wing   (wings)
A wing is one of the parts of a bird
or insect that it uses for flying. An
aeroplane also has wings.

winter   (winters)
Winter is the coldest part of the year.

---

wire   (wires)
A wire is a long, thin strip of metal
that can be bent easily.

---

wish   (wishing, wished)

When you wish,
you say or think
what you would
like to happen.

---

woman   (women)
A woman is a fully grown female
person.

---

won
See **win**.
I've won the game!

---

wood   (woods)
1 Wood is the material that comes
from trees. It can be used to make
things like furniture and paper.
2 A wood is a lot of trees growing
together.

a b c d e f g h i j k l m n o p q r s t u v **Ww** x y z

wool
Wool is the thick, soft hair that covers sheep. It is spun into thread and used for making cloth and for knitting.

word   (words)
Words are what you use when you speak or write. Words that are written have a space on each side of them.

wore
See **wear**.
I wore a heavy jumper yesterday.

work
Work is a job or something else that you have to do.

world   (worlds)
A world is the Earth or anything else in space that is like it.

worn
See **wear**.
My jeans are worn out.

worry   (worrying, worried)
When you worry, you keep thinking about something bad that might happen.

worth
If something is worth an amount of money, that is how much it could be sold for.
Dad's watch is worth thirty pounds.

wrap   (wrapping, wrapped)
When you wrap something, you cover it in something like cloth or paper.

wrist   (wrists)
Your wrist is the thin part of your arm where it joins your hand.

write   (writing, written)
When you write, you put words or signs on paper so that people can read them.

written
See **write**.
She has written a long story.

wrong
Something that is wrong is not right.
It is wrong to tell lies.

wrote
See **write**.
I wrote a letter to Grandma yesterday.

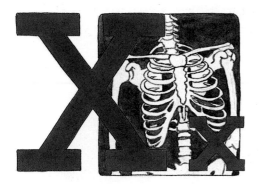

X-ray (X-rays)
An X-ray is a special photograph that shows the inside of a body.

xylophone (xylophones)
A musical instrument which you play by hitting the wooden or metal strips with small hammers.

zebra (zebras)
A zebra is an animal like a horse with black and white stripes. Zebras live in Africa.

zigzag
A zigzag is a line which bends suddenly one way and the other.

yacht (yachts)
A yacht is a boat with sails or an engine.

year (years)
A year is a measure of time. There are twelve months in a year.

young (younger, youngest)
A person or animal that is young was born not long ago.

zip (zips)

A zip is a way of joining two edges of material together. Some dresses, trousers, and bags have zips.

zoo (zoos)
A zoo is a place where different kinds of wild animals are kept so that people can go and see them.

a b c d e f g h i j k l m n o p q r s t u v w Xx Yy Zz

117

COLOURS AND SHAPES

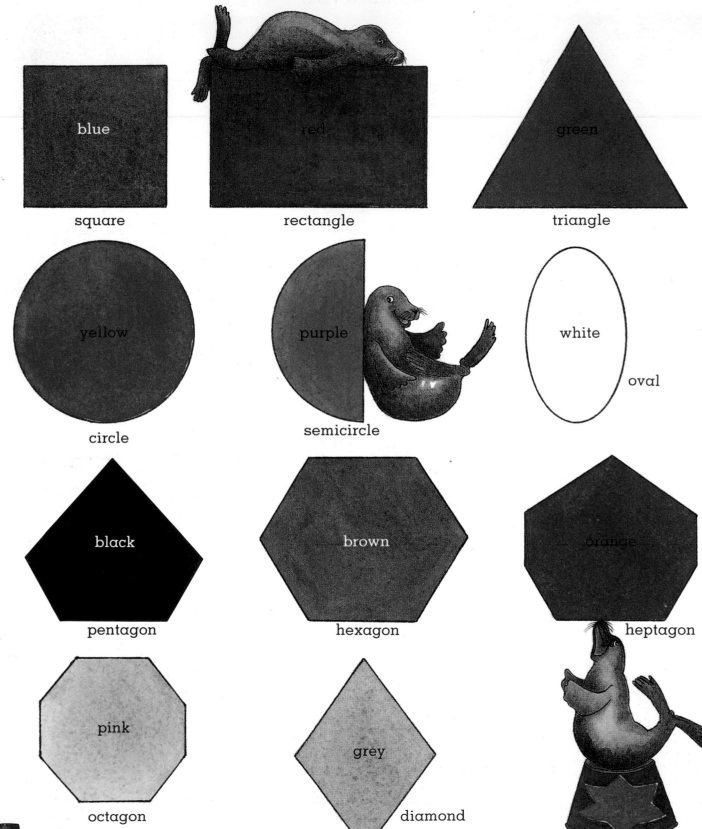

blue

square

red

rectangle

green

triangle

yellow

circle

purple

semicircle

white

oval

black

pentagon

brown

hexagon

orange

heptagon

pink

octagon

grey

diamond

118

OPPOSITES

large

small

fat

thin

hot

cold

old

young

long

short

inside

outside

few

many

wet

dry

old

new

happy

sad

open

closed

dark

light

119

FRUIT

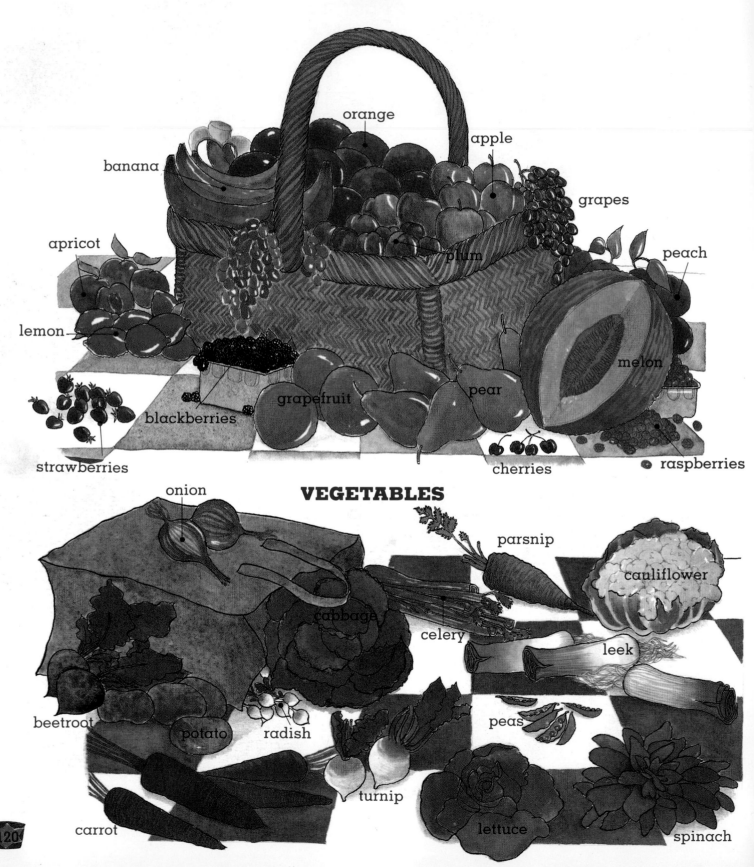

orange

apple

banana

grapes

apricot

peach

plum

lemon

melon

grapefruit

pear

blackberries

strawberries

cherries

raspberries

VEGETABLES

onion

parsnip

cauliflower

cabbage

celery

leek

beetroot

potato

radish

peas

turnip

carrot

lettuce

spinach

FLOWERS

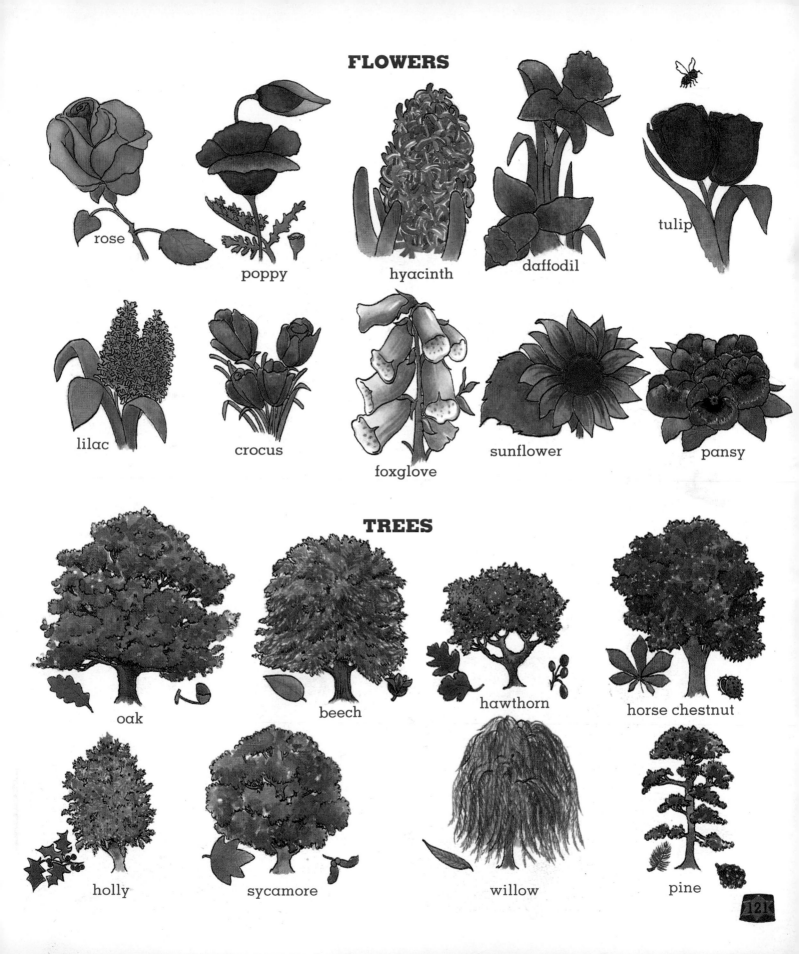

rose

poppy

hyacinth

daffodil

tulip

lilac

crocus

foxglove

sunflower

pansy

TREES

oak

beech

hawthorn

horse chestnut

holly

sycamore

willow

pine

121

ANIMALS IN THE WILD

polar bear

penguin

shark

whale

crab

parrot

elephant

zebra

lion

gorilla

snake

tiger

butterfly

beaver

beetle

spider

crocodile

panda

frog

DINOSAURS

Tyrannosaurus Rex

Triceratops

Stegosaurus

Diplodocus

Ankylosaurus

FARM ANIMALS

donkey

cow

goat

duck

horse

hen

pig

PETS

goldfish

budgerigar

rabbit

cat

dog

guinea pig

mouse

YOUR BODY

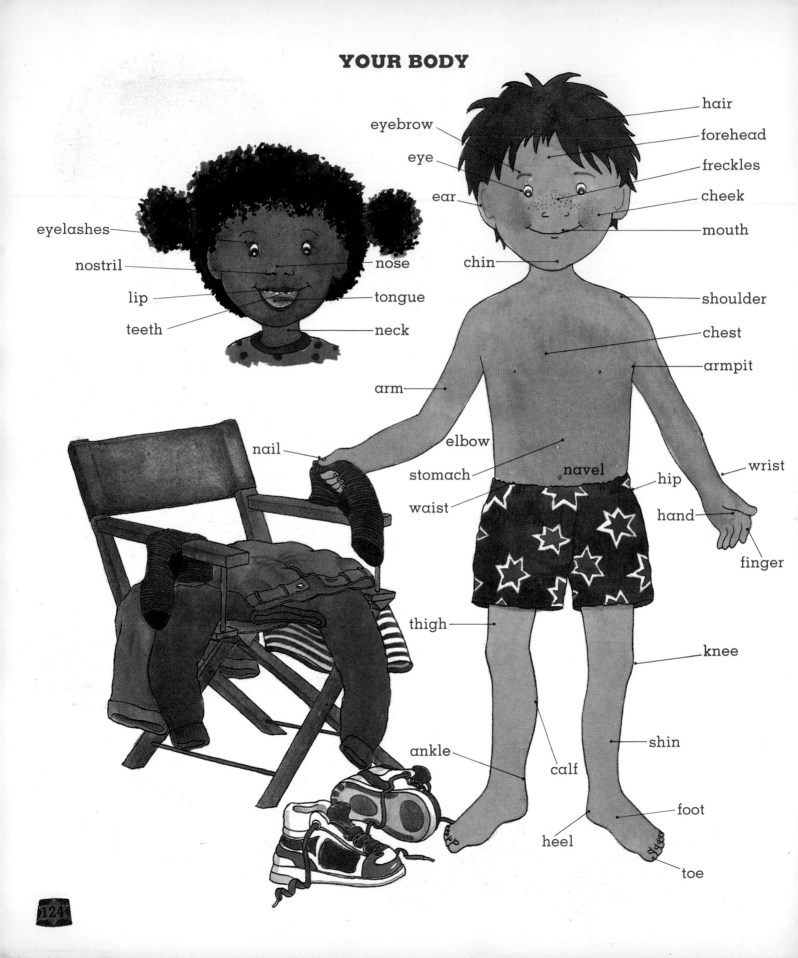

eyebrow

hair

eye

forehead

ear

freckles

cheek

mouth

eyelashes

chin

nostril

nose

shoulder

lip

tongue

chest

teeth

neck

armpit

arm

nail

elbow

wrist

stomach

navel

hip

waist

hand

finger

thigh

knee

shin

ankle

foot

calf

heel

toe

124

TRANSPORT

aeroplane

hot-air balloon

helicopter

yacht

ship

rowing boat

van

bus

bicycle

train

car

motorbike

TIME

 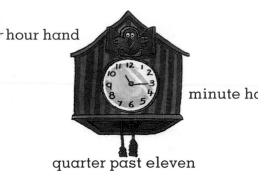

hour hand

minute hand

ten o'clock   quarter past eleven   half past one   quarter to two

SEASONS

spring

summer

autumn

winter

DAYS

Monday
Tuesday
Wednesday
Thursday
Friday
Saturday
Sunday

MONTHS

January
February
March
April
May
June
July
August
September
October
November
December

NUMBERS

1	one	first
2	two	second
3	three	third
4	four	fourth
5	five	fifth
6	six	sixth
7	seven	seventh
8	eight	eighth
9	nine	ninth
10	ten	tenth
11	eleven	eleventh
12	twelve	twelfth
13	thirteen	thirteenth
14	fourteen	fourteenth
15	fifteen	fifteenth
16	sixteen	sixteenth
17	seventeen	seventeenth
18	eighteen	eighteenth
19	nineteen	nineteenth
20	twenty	twentieth
21	twenty-one	twenty-first
22	twenty-two	twenty-second
30	thirty	thirtieth
40	forty	fortieth
50	fifty	fiftieth
60	sixty	sixtieth
70	seventy	seventieth
80	eighty	eightieth
90	ninety	ninetieth
100	a hundred	hundredth

WORDS WE OFTEN USE

a	could	her	or	too
about	did	here	other	took
after	do	him	our	up
again	does	his	out	upon
all	doing	how	outside	us
am	done	I	put	very
an	down	if	she	was
and	every	in	so	we
any	everyone	inside	some	went
anyone	for	into	take	were
are	from	is	taken	what
as	get	it	than	when
at	getting	me	that	where
away	go	more	the	which
be	goes	my	their	who
because	going	myself	them	will
but	gone	no	then	with
by	got	not	there	would
came	had	now	these	you
can	has	of	they	your
come	have	off	this	
comes	having	on	those	
coming	he	only	to	

FAMILY WORDS

mother	sister	daughter	grandmother	aunt
father	brother	son	grandfather	uncle
children	wife	granddaughter	grandchildren	niece
parents	husband	grandson	grandparents	nephew
cousin				